METS FAN

METS FAN

by Dana Brand

McFarland & Company, Inc., Publishers
Jefferson, North Carolina, and London

Four of the essays in this book, "For Shea," "Yankee Hatred," "Mr. Met," and "Marrying the Red Sox," first appeared on the author's website, *www.metsfanbook.com*. Another piece, "Mets Fan," also appeared on this website but was originally published in different form under the title "If You Prick a Mets Fan, He'll Bleed Blue and Orange" in the "Last Word" column of the Sunday Sports section of *Newsday*, August 28, 2005.

LIBRARY OF CONGRESS CATALOGUING-IN-PUBLICATION DATA

Brand, Dana.
    Mets fan / by Dana Brand.
        p.   cm.
    Includes index.

    ISBN-13: 978-0-7864-3199-1
    softcover : 50# alkaline paper ∞

    1. New York Mets (Baseball team)—Anecdotes.
    2. New York Mets (Baseball team)—Humor.   I. Title.
    GV875.N45B72   2007
    796.357'64097471—dc22   2007018672

British Library cataloguing data are available

Cover images ©2007 Shutterstock

Manufactured in the United States of America

McFarland & Company, Inc., Publishers
    Box 611, Jefferson, North Carolina 28640
        www.mcfarlandpub.com

To the Mets fans of the future,
including Sonia, Sam, and Sarah,

and to Helen and Lenny

Acknowledgments

My greatest debt, as a baseball fan, is to my family. Both of my parents grew up within walking distance of Ebbets Field and they loved the Brooklyn Dodgers. Having lost their team, Leonard Brand and Helen Thomashow Brand embraced the Mets. They taught me to love the rag-tag, gutsy, tolerant, generous, and hopeful spirit of New York that the old Dodgers represented and the Mets inherited. I am so grateful to them for this, as I am grateful for their many other gifts to me. My sisters, Jennifer and Stefanie Brand, have shared the Mets with me more than anyone else and when I go to a game with them, I feel as if I'm where I came from and where I belong. At Shea, with my daughter Sonia, I've enjoyed hot dogs, knishes, pretzels, Cracker Jack, and some of the most wonderful afternoons and evenings of my life. Along with my immediate family, I want to thank my extended family, particularly my cousins Byron, Mitchell, and Peter Thomashow. We were a Mets family, one of the millions of big family groups you could see in the 1960s on their blankets and in their cabanas along the beaches of Long Island, listening to Bob Murphy's voice on the radio.

My wife, Sheila Fisher, has encouraged my creativity and tolerated my baseball fandom over the years. A Red Sox fan since birth, she too loves baseball, but so deeply that she has not been able to return to it since the fateful evening of October 25, 1986. Sheila is the main pillar of my life and she is the best reader and editor of everything I write. She knows, better than anyone else, how this is a book about baseball and how this is a book about many things other than baseball. I thank her and I thank her family, Charlie, Shirley, and Sally Fisher, for teaching me about the similar and different universe of the Red Sox fan. Charlie, in particular, has helped me to understand what is shared by all baseball fans.

I also want to thank the many friends from all different parts of my life who have enjoyed baseball with me, who have gone to games with me, watched games on TV, or just talked with me or e-mailed me about this thing we all love so much. In roughly chronological order, I would like particularly to thank Michael Kastner, Rick Millington, John Anderson, Jonathan Freedman, Bart Giamatti, Harriet Davidson, Bruce Tucker, Lee Zimmerman, Paula Uruburu, John Bryant, Ginny Blandford, John Klause, Danny Kessler, and Alison Frankel.

Finally, I want to thank the people who contributed most directly to the creation of this book. I want to thank Philip Lopate who, after reading a personal essay I wrote on baseball, suggested that I send it to *Newsday*. When I did this, only half-seriously, it caught the eye of the very smart and literate Sports Enterprise editor, Michael Dobie. Michael edited my work with care, respect, and common sense. He made it better and *Newsday* published a shorter version of my essay as a column in the Sunday sports section on August 28, 2005, under the title "If You Prick a Mets Fan, He Bleeds Blue and Orange." The response I got to this piece was overwhelming. The real parents of this book are the hundreds of Mets fans who wrote to me, praised the piece or reposted it on the Web. Their enthusiasm and encouragement convinced me that there needed to be a book like the one I have done my best to give them.

I am enormously grateful to Chris Morehouse, Anne Marie O'Farrell, and Denise Marcil of the Denise Marcil Literary Agency for believing in the book and working so hard for it with such kindness, skill, and energy.

I hope I have done all these people proud. I hope I have spoken for millions of people I've never met. I hope you enjoy this book and I hope you find in it what you expect and some things you may not expect.

Table of Contents

TABLE OF CONTENTS

Preface

This is a book for fans of the New York Mets, and for baseball fans everywhere. I write about what the players on our team mean to us. I write about the good years and the bad years. I write about what Mets fans feel when we go to Shea, and see Mr. Met, or Cow Bell Man or the home run apple, when we see our logo, sing our song, or cheer for our team. I write about what we feel when we bring our kids to a game or when we watch the most important games in Mets history with the people we love. I write about what the Mets are in our lives, about how beautiful baseball is and how wonderful, exciting, sad, and horrible it can be.

I've tried to write the kind of book about the Mets that Mets fans deserve. They deserve a book that's well-written and funny and that explains what it is actually like and what it means to bleed blue and orange. I can't tell you what goes on in the Mets dugout or the clubhouse or the hotel bars or the front office. I don't have any idea what goes on there. But I think that you'll be able to identify with what I have experienced in the stands, on my couch in the front of the TV, or in my car as I've listened to the game sitting in traffic on the Grand Central Parkway. I want Mets fans to recognize themselves in me and I hope that fans of other baseball teams will recognize themselves as well.

So, actually, this is not just a book for Mets fans. It is a book about what it's like to be a baseball fan and about what it's like, simply, to be a fan. Nothing is like baseball. It is a big beautiful beast that would be happy to swallow you. It's a sport that leaves all this room for contemplation, for the imagination, for the intellect, and for the emotions. Being a fan is a way of living life. It is a way of surrendering to fortune, a way of loving, a way of feeling connected with the rest of the world. Fans have this thing they can't get rid of. It makes them miserable and sometimes it makes them about as happy as it is possible to be. Fans share something they love with people who are close to them, and with people they will never meet. Being a fan of anything is wonderful. And it has its problems and its limitations.

I hope you enjoy reading about what I've been through in my forty-five years as a Mets Fan. And I hope you enjoy whatever my book reminds you of in your own life.

Mets Fan

There is no good reason why I should care about the New York Mets.

Like all baseball teams, they are a business. I should care no more about their success than I care about the success of a movie studio or television network. Yet I choose to care, deeply and powerfully. I have cared about the Mets for 45 years and probably will for the rest of my life. I enjoy my loyalty. I enjoy the irrationality and intensity of my loyalty.

Although my allegiance is a choice, at a certain level, it is not. The Mets are part of my heritage. My parents grew up as Brooklyn Dodgers fans. Three years after I was born, their team was taken from them in a way that should have left them permanently disillusioned with baseball. But they weren't disillusioned when the Dodgers moved to Los Angeles. They wanted baseball back and they wanted me to have baseball, too. And they did not, under any circumstances, want me to have the Yankees.

As my interest in baseball awakened during the summer of 1961, my parents persuaded me to ignore the excitement of the race to break Babe Ruth's home run record. They persuaded me to ignore the first World Series of which I was aware. They persuaded me to wait to begin my lifelong love affair with baseball until the summer of 1962, when there would be a new National League franchise in New York, a team that would replace the Dodgers, a team that would represent the vast remnant of the metropolitan area that refused to be represented by the team from the Bronx.

The central pleasure of my first year of fandom was rooting for a brand-new team. I loved the novelty of the blue and orange colors, and the cool, contemporary brevity of the name. I loved the logo, a baseball encompassing the skyscrapers and bridges of New York. It was the only team logo that featured a city, and it was my city. I don't remember minding that they were a very bad team, the worst in modern baseball history. I loved them wildly and intemperately. Anything they accomplished was good, and everything about them was part of me.

The Mets were bad for all of my childhood, but I never lost hope. I dreamed of them winning the World Series the way I dreamed of winning a Nobel Prize, an Academy Award or a presidential election.

Then came 1969, unforeseen and soul-filling, and neither I nor millions of others have ever gotten over it. The Mets remained the Mets, ordinary people competing against giants, yet they suddenly seemed to have magical powers. Everything happened as I wanted it to happen, reliably, inexorably. The young pitchers were perfect. The hitters hit when needed. Mediocre fielders made spectacular catches. The Mets won game after game and did not stop.

For months, nearly every thought I had—every sweet, pleasurable thought—was of them. It was like being in love. I was too young to perceive the absurdity, and nowhere near old enough to value my emotion in spite of its absurdity. I simply enjoyed, and I never will forget how much I enjoyed the summer of 1969.

For fans of my age, the summer of 1969 is the defining myth of the Mets.

Yankees fans have their myth: The Yankees are invincible, the team of Ruth and Gehrig, the only team for whom a season is not a success if it yields only a pennant, for whom a bad season is an anomaly. The myth is a crock, of course. The Yanks have had plenty of mediocre seasons in the last 40 years.

The Mets' myth is the reverse. Mets fans tend to think of the Mets as a fundamentally bad team that, every once in a while, briefly and magnificently rises up to play against type. When the Mets win, the fans feel as if they themselves have willed the team forward. We were the ones, with our slogans and signs, who took a last-place team to a pennant in

1973. We were the ones who drove Mookie Wilson's ball between Bill Buckner's legs in 1986. We were responsible for Al Leiter's perfection in the one-game playoff against the Reds in 1999. And we made Shea Stadium thunder in 2000, frightening the superior Cards and Giants into submission.

Yankees fans do not feel responsible for what the Yankees do. But Mets fans feel that they create the atmosphere that allows miracles to happen. Mets fans live to be a part of miracles. And fans who live for miracles don't need the odds on their side. Mets fans don't need or even ask for triumph. They want astonished fun, and the mystical sense of power that a Yankees fan can't know. They want the pleasure of the unexpected, even of the undeserved.

This is what has hooked us. This is what we long for. This is why, however much we hate them at times, we love to love this team. However good the Yankees become, they never tempt us. We are stubborn and resolute. We are millions. We are Mets fans.

For Shea

The Mets, as I write, are building a new stadium in Flushing. It will be called Citifield and it looks as if it will be very nice. It will be smaller than Shea and it will resemble Ebbets Field. It will have wider seats and more legroom. And the playing field will be closer to the stands. Like most Met fans, I am impressed. Like many Met fans, I am ambivalent.

I know that Shea doesn't deserve to be mourned. But I will miss it terribly. I remember when it was young, when it opened besides the World's Fair, when it was part of the City of the Future. Who was to know that the real future would prefer Ebbets Field? Shea was so hopeful, with its big and bright modernity. It was decorated with ruffled pieces of blue and orange metal which were eventually taken down. These were replaced by fluid and gigantic neon sketches of players in action, which I always thought were bright and lovely on their surface of deep Mets blue. Shea looked all right on the outside, but nothing much could be done about all the bad ideas in the interior.

As soon as you walk into Shea, you don't know what you're inside of. You feel like you've been forgotten about, or perhaps eaten. Staircases, ramps, and escalators come out of nowhere and you can't see what they're attached to. There are no focal points or spaces, just lit ads and posters that someone seems to have put up a long time ago.

Sure the seats and rows are cramped, but I like them. You feel as if you're in the middle of other people's lives. You hear their conversations and nothing prevents you from joining them. You are along on the dates with the girls snuggling against the guys for warmth. The nut has to be lived with. The guy next to you on the edge of his seat can't sit still and therefore you can't either. At Shea you are attached to the crowd, physically and emotionally, and when people stand up and scream, you are pulled up with them because you can't pull away from them.

In the new stadium, I will probably like being closer to the action on the field. But I'm not really convinced that smaller is good. Try getting tickets for a game at Fenway. I like how big Shea is. I like it when it has 55,000 people in it. I like how noisy it can get. I like its awkward incoherent immensity, which never feels oppressive because so many things at Shea are so silly, like Mr. Met and the apple in the hat and the t-shirt launches and Lou Monte singing "Lazy Mary" at the seventh-inning stretch. Shea has a personality. It is big and goofy and unsophisticated. It inspires the stadium characters who come and go over the years, who make themselves famous by holding up signs or beating cow-bells. It inspires vendors and ushers to be characters. It inspires sentimentality and manic energy. It is very New Yorky in an old-fashioned way. The smaller, stylish stadium might preserve some of what Shea has. But I'll bet it won't be the same.

I love Shea. I can't help it. It's been a part of my life for over forty years. I will miss the name: a quick syllable. I will miss what I feel every time I approach the blue bowl wrapped in its web of highways. I love to drive into the parking lot where people are picnicking just to be near it. I love it in the sun and the wind, and I love it when the lights have turned the nighttime into magical bright green daylight. And I love it when the Mets have won the game in their last turn at bat, when the echoing exit ramps vibrate with the voices of thousands of people who can't stop chanting and cheering.

However much I love it, I can't even hope to make an argument for keeping Shea. My only argument is a selfish one. I don't want a new stadium because it won't contain my memories. Part of the reason I go to Shea is to visit my memories. I remember my childhood birthdays. I remember Tommie Agee hitting a leadoff home run into the edge of the upper deck. I remember Clendenon's long swing and Piazza's short swing. I remember Seaver's rising fastball and Strawberry's first game. I remember the intimate emptiness of the stadium in the lean years, the urgent carnival atmosphere of the good years.

When I go to Shea, I feel as if I am visiting my father and several long lost versions of my daughter. I visit all of the different eras of my life, and all of the different teams and players who gave me so much happiness as I grew up and grew older. So many pieces of my life are connected by the fundamentally unchanging experience of a game at Shea. So much of what I have known and been seems held in the great curved embrace of the stands, in the rich green symmetry of the field, in the chaos of girders and buttresses and bathrooms and frying food on the concourse behind the seats. So much of me is here, in this thing that can be torn down but can't be replaced.

Here is where all those seasons happened. Here is where we ran onto the field in 1969. Here is where the ball went through Buckner's legs. Shea is where I've been. I will miss it as I miss a parent or a grandparent. I know it has to go. But I wish it could have been there for all of my life. I will endure its passing, but I would have loved to have been an old man in these seats, under these lights.

Mr. Met

There is something automatically fascinating about a living creature with a face that doesn't change. Mr. Met has had a big baseball head for over 40 years, and he has had the same smile and the same unnerving, unblinking eyes. Mr. Met looks as if he always feels the same thing about you, and about everyone he meets. He is as happy to see adults who turn away from him as he is to see children who run to him. He is as happy to dance with Greeks as to dance with Pakistanis. Everything pleases him and nothing fazes him. He does not speak, but he loves to dance. He reminds me of the Laughing Buddha you see in Chinese gift stores. He may not have a big belly, but he has a very big head. And his perfect happiness makes you wonder if he will bring luck.

Mr. Met is the right host for the ballpark because he makes you feel goofy. He convinces you that an undiscriminating silliness is a precious state of being. He follows the people who shoot the t-shirts into the crowd and yes! you want a t-shirt. When he dances on the dugouts, you bounce your head from side to side. He is happy when the Mets do well and you are happy when the Mets do well. He raises his arms and you cheer.

He doesn't seem to be around when the Mets screw up. Where does he go? Do they hide him? What's the story with this? Is there a policy that requires him to stay in the clubhouse when things aren't going well? Is he in there? Smiling, happy, surrounded by glum and foul-mouthed ballplayers? That would be something to see. How does he make the players feel? Maybe he actually stays on the field but you just don't notice him.

You forget that someone is inside, someone who probably doesn't have that smile on his face. You forget that someone is paid to dance and to manage the big bobbly head. You don't think of Mr. Met as a guy in a suit. He seems real. He is as real as anything else at the stadium.

I see a part of myself in Mr. Met. I see a part that I need in order to be a baseball fan. I see the part that doesn't get upset, that keeps coming back for more and more, that is happy with everything he sees at the park from the moment he comes in to the moment he leaves. I see the part that lives with the lousy trades and bad decisions and disappointments and never thinks of rooting for a different team. I see the part of me that stays happy and content even while waiting in a line of cars to leave the big lot through the space in the fence that puts you out on the road with the shops that sell auto parts and hubcaps.

Meet the Mets

I love the original version of "Meet the Mets," the team song. I am so glad that people now sing it after the first inning at Shea. I love the way it sounds like something written to be sung by people with gleaming teeth. I love the way "the time of your life" is "guaranteed!" the way home runs are "those home runs!," the way we are all so happy that "everybody's coming down!"

The original version of the song makes the sexist assumption that "you" would bring your wife and not your husband or significant other to the ballpark, but this is part of the period flavor. At the end of what is sung, there's an instrumental portion for which words were written although they've rarely been heard. You know, it goes something like "Oh the butcher and the baker and the people on the street, where are they going? To Meet the Mets!!!!" I knew those words once because I sent away for them. This is the world of "Meet the Mets." New York City neighborhoods with butchers and bakers, hearty, husky guys in aprons and the people on the street with hats, all in the kind of animation you used to see during intermissions in drive-in movie theatres, the ones that tried to get you to go buy something at the snack bar. Everybody in a crowded clump, with the feet moving real fast. Where are they going? To meet the Mets!!!!

They updated the song at some point and they play the update on the radio before every game. Instead of the early '60s' chorus they have a woman "whoo-wahhing" it. The new version is shorter, as if people don't have the attention span for the old version. No longer do you bring kiddies or wives. Instead you are promised what sound like "hot dogs, bean bags, all out at Shea," which is really "hot dogs, green grass, all out at Shea." And you are "guaranteed to have a heck of a day!" Whoo-wahhh! I suppose the "heck" is a modern touch. Maybe there's an unexpurgated version of the song that is played in the bar of the Diamond Club that has a word in it that has to be watered down to "heck." I like the older version of the song a lot better.

It is so sweet and so tacky. So Mets. This isn't a song with which you charge to the top of the standings, or celebrate triumph or a glorious tradition. It is not a song for champions. They must have figured this, when they wrote it. You can hear in the song an understanding that an expansion team in 1962 could not get away with taking itself too seriously. It would need to get by on charm. It could not compel your respect or admiration. It would just have to be nice and a little corny. You would come and meet the Mets the way you would come and meet a nutty neighbor who put out a bowl of pretzels and a bottle of soda on a coaster on a table with too many magazines. You knew that the line about "knocking those home runs over the wall," was, well, not true.

Even when the Mets are good, I still think this is the right song for them. It has the New York thing with the "East Side, West Side." And it still has the I-can't-believe-I'm-hearing-this quality of an era when public relations was not a science. It fits with Mr. Met (who would think him up now?). It fits with the apple that comes up out of the hat every time a Met hits a home run. It doesn't come out of the twenty-first century and it doesn't have anything to do with winning baseball games. It's got the sound and feel of something that was supposed to be temporary but has become permanent, over the four decades. It is the tone of the team. It brings us back to the smiling sixties. It draws us into the Mets-happy universe.

Lets Go Mets!

As everyone knows, the Mets have a chant, "Lets Go Mets!" I don't know when it started, but I think it started at the very beginning. I even wonder if it may have been the first baseball team chant. That "Let's Go, Yankees" they have across town is obviously a rip-off. I don't think the Red Sox have a chant like this, or the Dodgers, or the Reds or the Cardinals. Of course I love it, as you would expect. I love the fact that each of the three syllables gets a beat. I love the way kids love it, as I did when

I was a kid. It is simple. Its "whack, whack, whack" meter lets you know right away that that's what the fans are chanting, and not something else. When the Mets are on the road, and Mets fans are in the stadium, its distinctive rhythm makes it so you can hear it, even if only ten people are chanting it.

How wonderful it is to have a team name that is only one syllable long and can be shouted at full volume. No other team has such a name. I like how it's "Let's Go," as if we're going along with them. Though no one ever writes it with an apostrophe. It's "Lets Go" not "Let us go." Go where? Are the Mets being addressed by the chant? Is it "Lets Go," you Mets? When you think about it, it's hard to determine exactly what the words are supposed to mean. It's more like a spell, or a blessing. It's an incantation rather than an exhortation. It means, "something good should happen." It means "we should win the game." It means the obvious. It means "Lets Go Mets!"

I like how Mets fans use "Lets Go Mets!" to end letters and cards and e-mails, or even to say goodbye. You don't think about what "goodbye" means either. It is a magic phrase to end an encounter. It is like Ciao! or Sholom Aleichem! or Cheers! It ends things with a statement of shared hope, of happy fellowship. It is only half-serious. But it's serious enough.

The Mets Logo

A couple of years ago, a Mets executive was quoted as saying that they were thinking of changing the Mets logo because it was "too busy." Of course, it's too busy. New York is too busy. It's the only logo that even tries to give you a sense that you are in a city where a team plays. It's the only logo that tries to suggest that a team represents a city, rather than a hat or a pair of socks or some birds.

The Mets logo is a baseball, with dark blue skyscrapers inside of it. Right over the skyscrapers, flying over what looks like the Brooklyn

Bridge, is the name "Mets" in bright orange script. The orange script is happy and cheerful. It is almost as tall as the skyscrapers. It would be hundreds of feet high if it were real. It looks proud to be flying over the Brooklyn Bridge, happy to be like a blimp gliding in front of the buildings. It looks like a friendly orange King Kong.

The logo gives you a sense that you're looking into a crystal baseball and seeing your home. It makes me think of the crystal ball that Glinda shows Dorothy. There's no place like home. It also makes me think of the miniaturized city from Krypton that Superman keeps under a dome in the Fortress of Solitude. That was his home. This is our home, this exciting place with tall buildings and bridges. It is our home, even if we live in the suburbs. Our team is the New York Mets.

Orange stitches stream and wind around the baseball just as the bridge stitches it all together at the bottom. How could anyone ever think of changing such a beautiful thing? When you see a batch of baseball logos, your eye immediately finds this one. It is the busiest. It's the most interesting. You could never call it obvious or forgettable. It is outrageous, in a silly way that has become familiar, and welcome, and beloved. It is still the bouncy new nut in the group. You see it, you wake up. You are excited. It can't be replaced. It looks like us.

Yankee Hatred

As a passionate New York Mets fan, I hate the New York Yankees. I root for any team that plays them. Only when the Yankees played Atlanta in the World Series did I stay on the sidelines. Every diehard Mets fan I've ever encountered feels the way I do.

I don't hate individual Yankees. I've enjoyed and respected players like Yogi Berra, Ron Guidry, and Bernie Williams. I admired the beautifully balanced and mainly homegrown team of the late 1990s. I feel a kinship with Yankee fans who stuck with their team from the mid '60s to the mid '70s, and the early '80s to the mid '90s. I think Joe Torre is terrific. The Yankees are part of the glory of the great American game. But I hate them anyway.

Of course, my Yankee hatred is a play hatred. I don't think differently about people depending on whether they root for the Yankees or the Mets. I realize that I would be a Yankees fan if my immigrant grandparents had settled in the Bronx and not Brooklyn. But even if it is just for fun, play hatred can be meaningful. Yankee hatred is an essential part of the emotional makeup of Mets fans. It intensifies the pleasure of Mets love.

In order to love the Mets, you have to want something that the Yankees cannot give you. The Yankees will give you, more reliably than the Mets, a team that will win. But to root for the Mets, you have to want to win in a certain way. Mets fans enjoy seeing themselves as fans of the underdog, impossible dreamers, as sentimental in retrospect about the lousy years as they are about the miracles of the good years. The miracles would not be miracles if the lousy years hadn't happened. And because of their history, and their eternal personality, the Mets always think of themselves as underdogs, even when they're good.

Yankee fans are sentimental too—about their dynasties. They weep with pride in the little graveyard out behind their left field fence. But because they define themselves by the dynasties, they resent the stretches of mediocrity that blemish their record of greatness. They don't have the amused, perverse love for the bad years that we have.

Yankee fans don't hate the Mets, because the Mets are not part of their story. To those who would be kings, the little people all blend together. The Yankees, on the other hand, are always part of the story of the Mets. They are the top dog that allows us to see the Mets as underdogs. The Yankees are not defined by the fact that they are not the Mets. But the Mets are defined by the fact that they are the New York baseball team that is not the Yankees. And Mets fans may be defined as the apparently irrational millions who could root for the Yankees, but have chosen not to.

There are people who insist that it is possible to root for both the Mets and the Yankees. These people are wrong. You can't root for both the Mets and the Yankees because each team offers a different portal into the pleasure of baseball. If you want what the Yankees will give you, it doesn't make sense to root for the Mets. They're failures, no fun. In order to love the Mets, you have to renounce any desire you have for the monotony of dominance. You have to think it's absurd to get excited about, or have your heart broken by a team that has won so many times. You have to cherish triumph because it is unexpected and rare. When John Sterling screams "The Yankees Win! The YAAANNNNNKKEEEESS WIN!!!!!!" you have to enjoy the contempt you feel for the idiocy of his exuberance.

Of course, Mets fans don't hate the Yankees all the time. We didn't hate the Horace Clarke Yankees or the Don Mattingly Yankees. We hate what we feel is the eternal essence of Yankee-ness, the triumphalism that blossoms during the dynasties, particularly the current one, which has lasted far too long.

In the last ten years, the Yankees have turned themselves into the kind of team any fan from any other team will naturally resent. Every time the ship springs a leak, it is plugged by a hall-of-famer. If someone plays badly, or someone is injured, Steinbrenner reaches for the wallet. The Yankees feel entitled. If they start a year off badly but make it to the playoffs, they aren't overjoyed. They are relieved.

It may not be fair for Mets fans to hate the Yankees for their wealth and dominance, since the Mets are a rich team too. Often the Mets have only been underdogs because of the incompetence of the front office. But since we share this city with the Yankees, and since we don't spend quite as much as they do, we feel a local version of what fans everywhere feel about the Yankees.

We wonder if Yankee fans can still be enjoying themselves. Can they experience the hungry hope that is baseball fandom for the rest of us? If they do still hope, aren't they gluttons? If they can still be disappointed, shouldn't they be embarrassed? I know the Yankees haven't broken any rules, but aren't they in danger of boring themselves to death? Haven't they reduced the payout for a jackpot to just a few coins?

The pleasure of being a Mets fan is that hitting the jackpot still feels the way it should. You hope. You lose. You lose some more. And someday you win. And you remember the pleasure of winning all your life. This is what baseball in a thirty-team professional league should be.

I hope the Mets never become like the Yankees. I want my baseball to be like real life, seasoned with failure and disappointment, ennobled by hope, and studded with just a few spectacular moments of pure joy.

1962

When people talk about the 1962 Mets season, it is customary to say that people filled the stands of the Polo Grounds in order to chuckle over the merry mishaps of lovable losers. Marv Throneberry, of the funny name, who missed touching a base once, looms large. So does the manager, Casey Stengel, who for all of his considerable baseball skills, is remembered for his clownish self-presentation and his rhythmic stream-of-consciousness style of speaking. There are always references to Casey's hijinks (what is a hijink?) and antics but I've never exactly known what they mean by that. The notion that the 1962 Mets were a comic ensemble has become so fixed in people's minds that even some people who were around at the time, and rooted for the team, remember them in this way.

But this is not the way it was. I was only seven years old at the time, but I'm pretty sure that this is not the way it really was. As I remember it, the fans took the 1962 Mets a lot more seriously than history has taken them. They were a baseball team and they were trying to win games and we wanted them to win games and we were not happy about those horrendous losing streaks. Sure, we didn't mind losing as much as we might have if we were rooting for a more established team. But however little we asked of the 1962 Mets, we wanted more for them.

As I remember it, Throneberry was not a particularly prominent player. He was there, of course, but we had no way of knowing that people in the future would think that he had such a funny name that they would always want to invoke him as the symbol of the funny season. We paid a lot more attention to Frank Thomas, who hit a thrilling number of home runs, more than any Met would until Dave Kingman. And we paid more attention to Roger Craig, a genuinely good pitcher, with the best pickoff move in baseball, who did not deserve the indignity of losing 24 games. The 1962 Mets were a decent group of guys and some of them, like Thomas, Craig, Richie Ashburn, and Al Jackson, were pretty decent ballplayers. And the ones who weren't very good had either once been great, like Gil Hodges, or else they were not really ready to play in the major leagues. It isn't a surprise that a team like this didn't contend. But we were rooting for dignity for this admirable bunch, and we were hopeful that in the years ahead, as the youngsters matured, they would have more than dignity.

I wish I could remember more of what happened in 1962, but as I said, I was seven. I remember when Throneberry missed the base and I remember my father asking me what all the noise was about on the radio and I remember telling him, without intending to make a joke, that Throneberry had hit a "sacrifice triple." My father thought that was so cute that he wrote about it to Ralph Kiner, who wrote back a sweet note of thanks, on the stationary of a Pittsburgh hotel, agreeing that it was a cute thing to say, and explaining how it would actually be scored. I still have and will always have the letter. I remember that the Mets were broadcast on WABC, which at that time was a rock and roll station. To this day, when I hear the luscious, heavily orchestrated rock and roll of the summer of 1962, I associate it with there being no game that day, or no game yet, or the game being over.

I remember triple plays, which were a specialty of the 1962 Mets. They were like four-leaf clovers. There hadn't been one for a long time but suddenly the 1962 Mets made a bunch of them. Or two or three, I don't know. The triple play has to be the most exciting play in baseball, and making them was something my team was good at. Sure, the 1962 Mets allowed so many base runners that they had more opportunities than other teams to make triple plays. But that didn't register with me. I was proud of everything they accomplished. I suppose I thought that they were like me. They were new and not yet competent enough to make much of a mark in the adult world. But they could do a few things well.

1962

I wish I could tell you the details of specific games, but I can't. I remember Thomas's home runs, Craig's pickoffs, and the triple plays. I also remember that we had a long reliever, Ken Mackenzie, who had a winning percentage above .500. I remember my parents, old Brooklyn Dodger fans, getting excited about Hodges and I remember wondering why he wasn't as good as they seemed to think he was. Most of what I remember are impressions. I liked the deep blue and hard candy orange Met colors. I liked the skyscrapers in a baseball logo. I liked the song, "Meet the Mets," and I managed to learn all of its verses (it's like the "Star Spangled Banner," most people don't know that it has more than one verse). I liked our sad little basset hound mascot, Homer. I liked the waltz-time jingle of the sponsor's song "My beer is Rheingold, the dry beer..." I liked the newness of the team. I liked having baseball and learning about baseball. I liked being seven and sharing something with adults that it seemed to me I could understand pretty much as well as they could. I liked walking on a street or in a shopping center, listening to the game on a transistor radio, and having grown men ask me what the score was. Grown ups never asked me questions to get information they didn't have, which they actually wanted to have. But when I had my radio, they did. I could tell them what they wanted to know and they would thank me. One weekend afternoon when I had my transistor radio in New York City, the Mets had scored something like 13 runs and I got to be the bearer of this news to several very appreciative strangers.

I really think that the 1962 Mets season was not quite what it has become. I suppose that is the case with anything that has happened in the past. I wish I could offer more proof of this but I can't. I remember what it was to me. My memories of 1962 stand at the gate, at the beginning of a lifelong relationship. And as is the case with anyone or anything with whom you have a lifelong relationship, what you know is not necessarily what most other people believe.

My First Game

The first baseball games I ever went to were the two games of a doubleheader played on September 15, 1963. I went to the game with my parents and my sisters, who were six and three, to celebrate my ninth birthday. These were the last weekend Mets home games of the 1963 season and they were the last weekend games ever played at the Polo Grounds, a stadium that had been built in 1890 and rebuilt after a fire in 1911.

It was, as I remember, so strange to go to a baseball game in a big building on a city street. From the fact that it was called a park, I had imagined that the stadium would be surrounded by a park, like a palace. It wasn't. It was right on the street and it was a big, old place with columns and an old-timey look that I liked and didn't like. I felt towards it the way I felt towards old people I didn't know well. I respected it for what it was, but it scared me a little.

I remember how bizarrely shaped the Polo Grounds were. The fences were very far away in center field and they were really close down the lines in left and right. If you hit a 300-foot home run in the Polo Grounds, Lindsey Nelson or Ralph Kiner or Bob Murphy would call it a Chinese home run. Obviously, they wouldn't call it a Chinese home run now, even if you could still hit a 300-foot home run. To this day, though, I don't know what made a home run like this Chinese. Was it because it was short, something a small person could hit? Was there some implication that it was tricky or cheap or sneaky? What a strange world that was. I still have so many unanswered questions. I wondered if the strange shape of the ballpark had something to do with the fact that it might have once been used for polo.

I brought my mitt, but no foul ball came anywhere near me. We ate in an old-fashioned deli in Washington Heights before the games, the kind with the waiters in the jackets where you can get Dr. Brown's sodas. This seemed appropriate. We left our house with the lawn in the suburbs to go to the ballgame in the city. It was an old-fashioned city experience, like visiting relatives in apartment buildings where they insisted on kissing you but wouldn't speak English. I liked it because it was interesting, but I was looking forward to next year, when there was going to be a brand new stadium out by the airports.

I think we lost both of those games, but I don't remember much about them. I remember how weird it was to see a baseball game, for the first time, played in silence, with no one describing it or commenting on it. People cheered and booed. That was the only commentary.

What I remember most about the games were all of the old men crying at the end of the second one. This was 1963 and I was only nine. I hadn't seen men crying very often. I'm not sure I had ever seen men cry at all. But there were a lot of them. I knew why they were crying but it was still something of a mystery to me. Didn't they realize that the new stadium was going to be better? In retrospect, I remember this as a weird prelude to what I would see two months after this, when the president was shot, and I would see a lot of men crying. That was a different kind of crying. At the Polo Grounds, there was no shock or surprise, and there were no women crying. There were men, standing in the seats at the end of a game, looking and squinting and crying.

That doubleheader was the first Banner Day. Between the games, everyone who had brought a banner was allowed to join a parade around the field. This was something to see. At some point it had become the custom to bring signs to the Polo Grounds, done with magic marker on oak tag, or with paint on old sheets. The signs had slogans and pictures. The idea was to be clever enough to attract the television cameras. The banners were a Mets "thing." They gave Mets games a distinctive atmosphere. Our expressions of love for our team were visual. They weren't just verbal. They were artistic. They were media-savvy. They made the game feel like a big march or a demonstration. In all these ways, the banners made the Mets feel very contemporary. When I was nine, I'd hear the word "New Breed" applied to the whole phenomenon of the Mets. I didn't understand if this was supposed to apply to the team or the fans. I took it as a reference to both. There was something new about all of this. And the sixties, as I was growing up in them, seemed to be about newness. I was new. The Mets were new. Everything in the sixties was new. There was nothing to cry about. So what if the old stadium was going to be torn down? Ebbets Field had been torn down. And my grand-parents now lived twenty floors above what had once been second base at Ebbets Field, in a modern apartment that still smelled of camphor and soup.

I'm amazed that my very first games were these games, when something so important was ending and something new was beginning. The stadium seemed impossibly old on that last weekend of its life. But it was only about fifty years old. It was not that much older than Shea is now. There must have been people there who had been in the stands when the rebuilt Polo Grounds opened in 1911. I've seen pictures of baseball games around that time, with men in straw hats, women in long dresses. Some of those people were still there, at my first game in 1963, watching the parade of the banners in front of the television cameras.

The Mets in the Sixties

However appealing the lovable Mets of 1962 may seem in retrospect, no one in 1963 wanted anything like 1962 to happen again. It had been proven that filling the roster with old guys was not a good way to win, even if it might have helped to fill the stands for a season. So the Mets tried a youth movement, and that made the Mets seem new all over again.

The best of the new young Mets was Ron Hunt, a 22-year-old second baseman. Hunt was the first good player who had never been anything but a Met. He came in second to Pete Rose in the balloting for Rookie of the Year in 1963 and in 1964 he was the first Mets player to earn a starting spot on the All-Star team. Hunt was exciting and aggressive and he could hit .300. By getting to a Safeway supermarket early one morning, I got a baseball autographed by him. I still have it.

I'm sad that you don't hear more about Ron Hunt when people talk about the history of the Mets. He doesn't fit easily into the story. He was our first good player, but the team was still bad. He was traded away before the Mets became any good. Mets history is now just 1962 and then

Tom Seaver comes in 1967 and things start to get better. But for those of us who followed the team from 1963 through 1965, Hunt was the big story. He suggested that if the Mets were ever going to become good, it would be because of young players you couldn't see coming, young players who would just appear and play well and excite you and get everyone's attention and respect. This is, in fact, how it would happen. We knew that a good second baseman wouldn't take us all the way. But we expected that a few other players of Hunt's caliber would emerge from the farm system, or to come in a trade. And so we kept looking for the next Hunt, the next piece of the puzzle, the Messiah.

My second and third favorite Mets in 1963 were Jim Hickman and Tim Harkness. When I look up their stats for that year (Hickman, .229, 17 hrs, 51 rbis; Harkness, .211, 10 hrs, 41 rbis), I'm amazed. I remember them being much better than that. I remember Jim Hickman hitting three home runs in a game, though maybe that was in a different year. I remember Tim Harkness hitting a grand slam home run in something like the fourteenth inning, with two outs and the count at three and two, and the Mets behind by two runs and thinking how this was the most exciting win imaginable, or would have been if the Mets had been behind by three runs. This is what I remember. This is what Hickman and Harkness were to me. This and the hope that such moments must have inspired. But I guess, looking at these numbers, that these moments weren't typical.

It's funny. When I look at rosters of more recent teams, I can remember what was good and bad about each player. I remember how and when and why they left the team. When I look at rosters from the time I was a kid, I remember all of the names. I remember my childish welcoming image of each player. But I don't remember them going bust. I remember that we lost a lot of games. But somehow the kid could not blame the players he loved so much. I don't remember having any clear idea of why the Mets were as bad as they were.

Part of me thought it was some kind of fluke. The most exciting thing that happened in 1963 was that the Mets beat the Yankees in the Mayor's Trophy Game, by a decisive score, something like 6–2. We could beat the Yankees. I know it was just an exhibition game and the Yankees said they didn't try very hard, but this was my first taste of baseball triumph. I will never forget it. And I thought it meant something.

Over the next few years, I got excited by Duke Carmel, Larry Bearnarth, Joe Christopher, Galen Cisco, Charlie Smith, Tracy Stallard, Johnny Lewis, and Dennis Ribant. It makes me happy to see the names of these obscure heroes in front of me all together again on my laptop. None of these was a new Hunt. And the Mets finished last every season except 1966 and 1968, when they finished ninth. But I paid a lot of loving attention to my team. After a while, I don't think I expected them to get better. There was something numbing and hypnotic about how every new guy who came along was just as good or bad or disappointing as the guys who went away. Swoboda was the same thing as Hickman. Hiller was the same as Kanehl. The older Kranepool was the same as the younger Kranepool. I got locked into a sense that the Mets couldn't get any better. They weren't professional athletes. They were just my guys. This was a cozy niche. I didn't expect miracles. I just expected the Mets. I really don't know how long this could have lasted.

Now when people think back on the Mets in the sixties, they can't remember what this time period felt like to people who did not know how the story would turn out. I can't remember this either. The Mets fans in the sixties are now remembered as wildly enthusiastic New York characters, with their signs and their cheers and their hoarse-voiced passion. They are remembered as happy, but deluded, and therefore deserving. We think of them now as wanderers in a desert, who don't know how much longer they're going to have to wander around. They don't know what is going to happen next. They do not understand that their suffering, their haplessness, their incomprehensible content with their sorry lot, is going to make them worthy of something of which they do not even dare to dream.

1969

The 1969 season will never go away. It gives a particular flavor to life, and it will be taken as a treasure to the end. No one could have foreseen what we saw. It stands apart from all other sports miracles. Baseball historians can point to a few examples of teams leaping from terrible to great in a single year. But none of these are comparable to the 1969 Mets because no other suddenly great team had spent so long in the cellar, and no other team had ever become such a symbol of futility.

Nineteen sixty-nine began like all of our other seasons, with a loss on Opening Day. We lost to an expansion team, the Montreal Expos. Nothing was surprising in April or May. Our pitching was good and our hitting was weak, just as they had been in 1968, when we poked our heads into ninth place. The Mets seemed to be headed for the fifth-place finish in a six-team division that everyone had predicted for them in the first year of divisional play and the first year of the Expos. But around Memorial Day, something happened that at the time seemed as weird as the discovery of crop circles or a story of an alien abduction. The New York Mets won eleven games in a row.

I remember how this felt. Something had cracked. The Mets had never done anything like this. When a team wins eleven games in a row, it alters your sense of what is possible. At the end of that eleven-game streak, the Mets were five games above .500. It was June, and my eye didn't need to look for my team at the bottom of the list. They were in second place. And for the very first time in my eight years of looking at the standings, the two-digit number on the left was larger than the two-digit number on the right.

Suddenly the Mets could imagine that they were in a pennant race, with the Chicago Cubs of all people, another Cinderella team emerging from years of mediocrity to dominate a division that everyone thought would have been dominated by the Cardinals. The Mets held steady. The Cardinals slept. And then in July, the Mets played the Cubs in the first series they ever played that actually mattered. They played it for all it was worth. In the first game, they came from behind in the bottom of the ninth. Seaver almost pitched a perfect game in the second. Then the Mets flubbed the third game with fielding errors, prompting Cubs manager Leo Durocher to call the clumsy team he was finally able to beat, "the real Mets."

This crack, from Durocher's lip, opened the floodgates. The worried Cubs despised us, and we would hate them back. Here were America's two biggest and oldest baseball cities. Here were two teams of great character, and no history of success. Only one could win. It was a shame. But boy it was fun. It was tense and it was wild, and as the season progressed it turned into a full-scale carnival, with brushback pitches, black cats, and taunting cheers. It was hand-to-hand combat between two desperate and deserving dreams. In the second Cubs series in July, at Wrigley, the Mets once again won two out of three. They were only three and a half games out of first place. In the middle of July.

Then it all collapsed. It had to. How could it possibly have happened? How could we have dared to hope for this? By mid–August, after a rough month, the Mets were nine and a half games behind the Cubs. They were in third place, as the Cardinals had finally woken up. And the Pirates were gaining. We would probably finish fourth. It was okay. This season had been more fun than any Mets season had ever been. I wasn't crushed. I was only 14, but I knew something about how the world worked.

I don't know how to describe what happened next. It is the best baseball memory I have. Imagine lightning. Imagine the silence after the flash. Imagine a swell of sustained thunder. Imagine the heavens opening and the rain loud and sweeping and drenching the earth. Imagine a baseball team winning thirty-eight of its last forty-nine games. Imagine all of the other teams crumbling with fear, dissolving into irrelevance. Imagine two young aces winning eighteen of their last nineteen starts. Imagine a team that has always been bad suddenly playing as no team ever has. Imagine the largest city in the world fully in its thrall. There are no words adequate to this. There are not even numbers.

There is only the bursting of all boundaries. There is only the image of thousands of fans spilling over the line that had kept them off the field on which the miracle has happened. There are flying corks and foam on the camera lens. There is the emotion of millions watching the Mets in their wet dugout singing all of the baseball songs they can think of. There is the memory of the hung-over Mets recording the songs in a studio the next day and all of us rushing out to buy the quickly-pressed record. There was a pure and powerful happiness that waved a wand over the previous seven years. The bad years would no longer be laughed at, or cried about. They were lifted up out of the gutter and given a place of honor at the table. They gave the moment of triumph its luster. They had been the preparation for the launch. They had been worth it. But you only knew it now. Everything had happened as it was supposed to happen. The Mets were not about living with failure. They were about the sweetness of victory after years of defeat. This was the real meaning of the Mets.

After the Mets won the NL East and celebrated, you needed to remind yourself that, for the first time in history, the team that had won more games than any other in the league still had to win a few more to claim the pennant. It's hard to believe, after the way they had played, but the Mets were still not favored to beat the Braves in the National League playoffs. It was as if nothing they could do could render what they had done believable. But the Mets beat the Braves quickly and easily, in only three games. But even that didn't make them favorites to win the World Series. The 1969 Baltimore Orioles were one of the best teams of all time. I wasn't in a mood to be greedy. I was happy with the pennant.

In those days, the World Series was played in the daytime. This made it a public event. You could see what it really meant to people. There were radios in every classroom and every office. You could hear the game in every street and every shopping center. It seemed as if the Mets were all that anyone anywhere was talking or thinking about.

Seaver lost the first game of the series against Baltimore. Seaver lost. Our team did not look frightening. None of them could hit like Frank Robinson and none of them could field like Brooks Robinson. Some of them could pitch as well as Mike Cuellar, but not this time. How had the Mets managed to win so many games? I felt, at the end of the glum and sobering first game, as if I was beginning to forget.

But the second game reminded me. The Mets won by scoring more runs than the other team. But just barely. To do this with their lineup, they had to have spectacular pitching. They got it this time. Koosman almost pitched a no-hitter. Clendenon hit a home run. The Orioles tied the game. But the Mets, with three little singles, went ahead in the ninth, and held it.

In the third game, the Mets win was decisive, the only decisive win of the Series. Gentry and Ryan combined for a shutout. Tommie Agee made two catches that have changed my understanding of how the human body can move. The Mets won, 5–0. They had the momentum again, and the rumbling sound you had heard all season long was back and it seemed as if it had never gone away. It swelled as Seaver returned to form in the fourth game, as Clendenon hit another home run, and as Swoboda, stinky fielding Swoboda, made a tumbling catch as great as either of Agee's the day before. In the tenth inning, a fated and probably wrong base-running call gave the game to the Mets.

The Orioles struggled mightily in the fifth game. They knew they did not deserve to lose. They could not understand what was happening. Surely, the Orioles must have thought, this thing could be prevented. They had eyes and minds and arms. They had will. And so they scored three runs before the Mets could do anything. Then in the bottom of the sixth, Cleon Jones reached first because Gil Hodges convinced an umpire that the shoe polish on a ball belonged to him. Clendenon hit another home run. Al Weis, who could not hit home runs, hit one to tie the game in the seventh. A wave came out of the crowd and pushed the Mets in front in the eighth. Human beings could not stop this, or anything else that had to happen. Davey Johnson would someday become the most successful manager in Mets history. But now, with two outs in the ninth, the Orioles second baseman hit a line drive to left.

In what seemed like slow motion, Cleon brought the dying ball into his glove. He squeezed it tightly. He dropped to his knees.

Tom Seaver

Tom Seaver was great and he knew it. That was part of what it was to be Seaver and no one should resent him for it. There is no rule that great ballplayers have to be insecure or modest. Part of what made Seaver great was that he was neither. He was in control and you have to admire someone who never loses it, who is always on, someone who bends the world to his will, and controls his universe as consistently as Seaver controlled his. He'd have his brief, vulnerable period at the very beginning of a game, until he found his groove for the day. But as soon as he found it, it was over. He had fastballs that could go anywhere he wanted them to, that could even appear to rise, in defiance of the laws of physics. He had slippery curves and sliders, and change ups that no one could see coming. Nothing hung, nothing was in the wrong place, nothing bad would ever happen, except for one or two times when he was hurt and keeping his mouth shut. The pleasure of Seaver's steadiness was great. Seaver would pitch and Seaver would win. And if he didn't, it would not be his fault.

Year after year, Seaver would pitch a 20-win season, whether he won 20 games or not. Year after year, his E.R.A. would be around 2, among the lowest in the league. Year after year he would strike out well over 200 batters and the number of his hits and walks combined would be just about equal to the number of his innings. It wasn't just that Seaver had magnitude. He was also steady. Other players could reach his level from time to time. But it seemed as if no one but him could reach his level and just stay there.

Seaver acted as if there was nothing unexpected about what he accomplished. He acted as if he knew what to do, and he knew how hard he had to work to do it. His inspiring arrogance was not the cocky, blue-collar arrogance that baseball fans often enjoy. It was a white-collar arrogance. Seaver was a thoughtful and educated man who seemed to approach pitching with the intellectual confidence and enthusiasm of the engineers who were landing people on the moon. He had the air of a bright young captain, not a tough grunt.

Seaver's debut in 1967 was the beginning of the end of the slapstick period of Mets history. Finally, our team had a Rookie of the Year, a player everyone in the league had to take seriously. The only really good players the Mets had had before Seaver were Ron Hunt, Ken Boyer, and Tommy Davis. But Hunt was traded for Davis and Boyer and Davis were just very good players nearing the end of their careers. When Seaver came up, the Mets finally had a legitimate star to build a team around, and so it seemed perfectly natural the next year when another star, Jerry Koosman, emerged from the farm system. After Koufax and Drysdale, it seemed as if double aces were necessary if you wanted to win a championship with pitching. Seaver and Koosman had a perfect complementarity. One was a righty and one was a lefty. One was particularly pleased with himself and one was self-effacing. They were like Koufax and Drysdale, twin pillars, solid and stunning, but unlike the Dodgers they were so incredibly young. It was exhilarating to see two guys who were so good and so young and so happy to be so good and so young. They were the real inner workings of the vaunted miracle. There was nothing supernatural or merely lucky about what happened in 1969.

Every Mets fan over a certain age remembers Tom Seaver's almost perfect game against the Cubs in July of 1969. It seemed to me, as it was happening, that no one had ever pitched such a pure and beautiful game. I remembered Jim Bunning's perfect game against the Mets on Father's Day in 1964. That was good, but hey, it was against the 1964 Mets. Seaver, on the other hand, was pitching perfection against an excellent team, a team that had a right to a pennant that year. But the Cubs couldn't do anything at all. They were small creatures in the big hands of a giant. Every Mets fan who saw that game can still feel what they felt when Jimmy Qualls hit a clean single into left with one out in the ninth inning. I guess it doesn't matter. Someone who wins 25 games and has an E.R.A. of 2.21 has had a historic season. Nothing was lost. The Mets won the game. But why do I think of that evening almost forty years ago so often? I think it's because that thing that was perfect should be there and no one should remember Jimmy Qualls. Part of the story of that miraculous year should be that one moment of perfection.

My next greatest Seaver memory is the game in which he struck out nineteen, breaking Sandy Koufax's record for strikeouts in a game. At the end of that game (at the end!) he set a record that still stands by striking out ten consecutive batters. This was one of the things about Seaver. He was perfectly steady and always good but there were games when he was like no one else, when he was sublime, alone with Sandy Koufax and Lefty Grove and Grover Cleveland Alexander. When this kind of thing happened, it was like hearing Caruso or Callas. It was as if something had come down to earth that isn't normally here.

As Gibson and Marichal began their decline, someone, at the end of the sixties, had to emerge to claim the title of baseball's best pitcher. Seaver came and took it. There was competition of course, but Palmer was just short of Seaver's level, and although Carlton could reach that level, he could not perform at it consistently. And so, as amazing as it had been for the Mets to win the World Championship, it was also amazing to realize that the Mets finally had one of those rare players who will be remembered forever, who has been the best in his era, the sort of player to whom future aspirants to greatness can be compared. Seaver was the best pitcher of the 1970s. He was the best player ever to rise through the Mets system. He was the best player ever to play for the Mets. And when he was traded to the Cincinnati Reds on that dark night in June of 1977, for no good reasons, only for the kind of stupidity and cocky conservatism and meanness that deservedly forgotten and superseded people like M. Donald Grant and Dick Young represented, it was the worst thing that had ever happened to the fans of the New York Mets.

We lost Seaver for five of his great years. The years should have been ours, but they belonged to the team with which we had fought so bitterly for the 1973 pennant. As Seaver approached 40, he came back to us. He could still pitch well. He was still worth watching, but even our new and better management and ownership could not avoid making one last blunder to further spoil an already spoiled fairy tale. Seaver wasn't protected in the 1983 free agent draft. He won his 300th game at Yankee stadium pitching for the Chicago White Sox. Instead of being able to remember him in our dugout as the Mets rose from the ashes in the middle of the eighties, we can now only remember him ending his career sitting unused, watching without expression, a big "B" on his cap, in the visitor's dugout in the 1986 World Series. The one man who could have and should have spanned our two great eras was deprived of his chance to do so first by the evil and then by the carelessness of management.

When his career was over, we retired his number. And everything that had not gone right about Tom Seaver's relationship with our team was glossed over and willfully forgotten. His "41" is on our left field wall, the only player's number ever to be retired. He is still spoken of as "The Franchise," as the greatest Met of all. He represents our past glory, as our first and last home-grown Hall-of-Famer. But like most of Mets history, his is not a well-managed or satisfying story. The pleasure of being a Mets fan comes from the wild accidental moments of grace. It comes in spite of what management does. It comes from surprises at the right moments, like the appearance of this bright, eager, and confident kid on our battered mound, just as we were beginning to grow tired of losing.

Jerry Koosman

Tom Seaver and Jerry Koosman reminded me of Napoleon Solo and Ilya Kuryakin. They also reminded me of Captain Kirk and Mr. Spock. This was a sixties pattern. And for young fans at the time, it was a very natural one. For any endeavor you needed a classic square-jawed hero, smoothed by a little sixties irony, but still very much at home in the limelight. You also had to have a sidekick, who was just as competent as the hero but with different skills. And the sidekick didn't want center stage. He was more shy. You had to seek him out. And this made him a little cuter.

Though Koosman was definitely Ilya or Spock to Seaver's Solo or Kirk, he didn't have the nerdy bohemian edge of Ilya or Spock. He was a genuine Midwestern farm boy. That's even more exotic in New York than moody Russian secret agents or Vulcans, but it is not as if there's anything intrinsically unsuited to New York life about Midwestern farm boys. Plenty of Midwestern farm boys have thrived in New York. Some even thrive while remaining Midwestern farm boys. Jerry Koosman was one of these. He had a wonderful sense of irony about the farm thing. He told the credulous big city reporters in '69 that he hadn't had so much fun since his third-grade picnic. He told reporters that he stayed in shape in the winter throwing in the barn to his brother Orville. I'm going to bet he didn't have a brother named Orville.

Koosman was tall and gangly (remember when pitchers were gangly?) He had the sweetest face imaginable. All eyes and cheeks and ears. No one who looked like that or smiled like that could possibly be a bad guy. Koosman looked like the tall, gawky, humble GI, away from home for the first time, who gets killed in the war movie. He was kind and humble, but he was also tough. Jerry was famous for the way he protected his teammates when other pitchers threw at them. He was a fine young man, but his curveball had no mercy and his precise inside pitching could carve a hitter's guts out.

For his first two years, Koosman was just as good as Seaver. They were together at the top and they seemed to enjoy being equals. They had their own routine going in the locker room, which the reporters called the "Tom and Jerry" show. In the beginning, Koosman wasn't really in Seaver's shadow. He was the second guy because Seaver made the team first, and because Seaver put himself forward a little more. After he hurt his elbow in 1970, Jerry dropped down a notch. But he came slowly back, just in time to help win the 1973 pennant. He had better seasons than Seaver in 1974 and in 1976. When Seaver came back to Shea for the first time as a Red, I went to the game and as much as I loved Seaver, I rooted for Jerry to beat him. The stadium was full, in 1977! Everyone cheered their heads off for both of them. It was all so terribly sad and unnecessary.

Jerry remained ours for two embarrassing years after Seaver was traded away. He pitched well, but he lost 15 and then 20 games. Still, he was always a trouper, always a Met and always humbly abashed at the intensity of our love for him. He didn't complain. At the end of the 1978 season, we were glad that the Mets had the decency to trade Jerry to Minnesota to end his career. After giving us eleven wonderful seasons, he would now be able to finish up near the farm, near his Mom, maybe near a brother named Orville, in the land of tall, upstanding people. We were mad when Jerry won 20 games the next year for the Twins. We were also mad when he went on to pitch for seven more years, and not just for the Twins, but for the White Sox, and the Phillies, who were not a hell of a lot closer to the farm and Mom than we were. We were mad, but we were mad at the Mets, not at Jerry. Never at Jerry.

Maybe Jerry was too humble. When you look at his career, he was number two a lot more than he deserved to be. In 1968, he had a better rookie season than Johnny Bench, but Bench won Rookie-of-the-Year by half a vote. In 1969, Jerry probably deserved to be the World Series MVP, but Donn Clendenon was chosen. In 1976, Jerry certainly deserved to win the Cy Young Award. He had a better record, a better E.R.A., and twice as many strikeouts as Randy Jones, who won it. The Mets have retired Seaver's number, but they haven't retired Koosman's, even though Koosman pitched almost as many innings as Seaver and was almost as good. Seaver has, of course, made the Hall of Fame. Koosman hasn't. But he had as good a career as Don Drysdale, Ferguson Jenkins, or Catfish Hunter, all of whom are in Cooperstown. If he hadn't pitched for years for hitless Mets teams, he would have had more than 250 wins, instead of just 222. You can't help but wonder if Jerry's good humor and humility have convinced people that it's okay not to give him honors, because he doesn't expect it. He's always okay. It drives me nuts.

He may not expect it, but like all Mets fans who remember him, I want to push Jerry Koosman into the circle of a spotlight to take a bow. He was a sweet, wonderful guy to root for, and he was a great talent and a real competitor. The world has taken him for granted. But we don't. Mets fans don't.

1973

In each of the three seasons after 1969, the Mets won exactly 83 games. Was this consistency? No. Was this mediocrity? No. The Mets were still the 1969 team. They could have been great. Clendenon was even better in '70 than he had been in '69. Seaver was consistently spectacular. Jerry Koosman had come down a level, with his bad elbow, but other pitchers were getting better. Cleon Jones and Tommie Agee had their ups and downs, but they could still play as they had in '69. There wasn't any reason why this team that had done it once couldn't do it again.

The memory of 1969 lingered liked the flavor of champagne (mingled with sweat and served over the top of the head). Nothing could have kept up the intensity of 1969 and no conceivable season could have been as miraculous. But the afterglow was there. In each of the next three seasons there were moments when you felt that the Mets would win it again. They were in first place or close to first place almost all the way through the 1970 season. In 1971, they were in the thick of it until the All-Star break. In 1972, the Mets got off to their best start ever, holding first place through all of April and May, in spite of having lost Gil Hodges, their beloved manager, to a heart attack on a golf course. But in '72, as in '71, and as in '70, things happened: injuries, mysterious slumps. By the time the season ended, there were the same 83 wins staring us in the face, and the same third-place finish. We couldn't escape. It was like the movie *Groundhog Day*. And what made it particularly weird was that our new manager was the man who was famous for having actually said that something was déjà vu all over again.

Nineteen seventy-three was déjà vu all over again in spades. It was the pits. There had been hope in the beginning because the team was genuinely improved. Koosman was getting his fastball back. The great Jon Matlack was with us now, and Rusty Staub was having his first full year as a Met. It seemed as if the Year of the Hammer might have finally arrived as John Milner began to play like a star. Even though there were new players, we still had the sense that we were rooting for the '69 team. We were in first place at the end of April. But then it was as if a bomb had been detonated in the clubhouse. There were something like seven men on the disabled list. Key players like Harrelson and Grote were out for months. By August, the Mets were ten and a half games out of first place, thirteen games under .500. We were just waiting for the season to end. It was true that none of the other teams in our division was playing particularly well. But one of them would have to get hot in September. One team would have to finish in first. It just wasn't going to be us, down there under the pile.

Every Mets fan of a certain age can remember what they think they saw next. One person is given the credit for turning the 1973 season around and giving the Mets their second miracle. Tug was a nut. He was an emotional left-handed relief pitcher. He had been great in 1969, 1970, 1971, and 1972. But he was lousy all through the summer of 1973. The story goes that one day in August that moron M. Donald Grant decided to motivate the team by giving them an undoubtedly inarticulate and clueless pep talk. At the end of the talk, Tug McGraw, who was smart enough and low-paid enough to have probably hated Grant's guts, started dancing around saying something like "You're so right, Mr. Grant, ya gotta believe!" Grant thought Tug was mocking him and he probably was, although he later denied it. But take a phrase, even if it's ironic, take a room full of New York reporters, take a city full of Mets fans forever affected by their memories of 1969, take a perfect focal personality like Tug McGraw, crazy, handsome, and suddenly pitching better than any left-handed reliever in history, slapping his thigh with his glove at the end of every terrific inning, and what do you have? You have the 1973 National League pennant. You have it just barely. But you have it.

Others contributed of course. Wayne Garrett, who looked as if he just stepped off a raft, and couldn't hit for either average or power, suddenly hit for a lot of both. The mighty Rusty hit with an authority that suggested that he knew that this was the way it was supposed to happen all along. Cleon Jones came through like the cavalry. Seaver was Seaver, Koosman was Koosman, and Matlack was better than Gentry had ever been. And if anyone got into any trouble, there was Tug, as if possessed, as if his eyes were glowing, getting 12 saves and 5 wins in his last 19 appearances. Stirred by the demon reliever, and by his slogan, and by the sign man at Shea who had so many opportunities to hold it high over our screaming heads, the fans were right in the thick of it. We gave them the power. We pushed them. And in the last week of the season, the Mets crawled over the .500 mark. At the very end, they were on top, with 82 wins. A rain-out had kept them from winning the magic 83rd game. The spell had been broken.

In the playoffs that year, the Mets faced a team that felt that we did not belong in the same ballpark with them. We understood. We had finished seventeen games behind them. But the rules were the rules and we knew, and they knew, that however great the 1973 Reds were, we had a better pitching staff. In the first game, Seaver was fabulous, but Rose and Bench beat us with homers. In the second game, Matlack pitched a two-hit shutout. We were reminded of the series against the Orioles, where Seaver had been beaten in the first game and Koosman had come back to pitch the game of his life.

The Mets clobbered the Reds in the third game and the frustrated Pete Rose, to break up a double play, ran into Buddy Harrelson covering second base. He ran into him so hard that we wanted to kill Charlie Hustle (what a stupid nickname). The good thing was that the Mets wanted to kill him too. Over our boos, the Big Red Machine managed a 2–1 victory in game 4. But in the fifth game, we clobbered them again, 7–2, to win the pennant.

When we won, the fans swarmed the field. Obviously, fans shouldn't do this, and no one does it any more. But this had been glorified by the press in 1969, as an image of the miracle. In 1973, the fans wanted everything to be exactly as it had been in 1969. Of course this wasn't possible. Of course you couldn't have this twice. And so the press decided to do something different this time. What had been represented as glorious in 1969 got painted as sinister and threatening in 1973. Even though no one was hurt, and the joy was just as generous and genuine, the Reds were able to point to the swarming fans as proof that they had a moral right to the pennant they hadn't won. Sparky Anderson wondered if New York was really in America. Our enemies always wonder this. After 9/11 they're not allowed to say it anymore. But they still wonder. And we keep them guessing. The offended Pete Rose compared Mets fans to animals who had been let out of a zoo. Thirty-three years later, I spit on him, and on his sorry legacy. Oh, I forgive him and all and I think that he should be in the Hall of Fame. That's just the way he was. But I still remember him in the fight that followed his "slide." I remember him sitting on top of Harrelson, swinging away, and my blood pressure rises more than thirty years later, and so I spit on him: the gambler, the crook, the bully.

Things got back to normal for the World Series, which felt more like a circus than a struggle. Part of it was because the Athletics were so strange. They were terrific, of course, but they were bizarre. They wore these seventies interpretations of old-timey uniforms and they had handlebar moustaches and they looked as if they were trying to be the 1910 Fruit Gum Company. They also had a crazy owner, Charlie Finley, who tried to get his second baseman's head examined after he had made two decisive errors in the second game. The Mets and the Mets fans never really got a fix on the A's. They were like something in a dream. They won one and we won one. They won another and we won one right back. Then we went on to take a 3–2 edge in the series, with Seaver and Matlack scheduled to pitch the last two games. We should have won one of those two games, and we almost won the first one. But we didn't win either. The season ended for us in the seventh game of the World Series. That was sad. But not so sad for a team that had been in last place on August 30.

Nineteen seventy-three was not 1969. But it was a kind of aftershock. A ripple. Once again we got to see Seaver, Koosman, McGraw, Agee, Jones, and Kranepool in a pennant race, in a championship series, and in the World Series. Something that could never happen again happened enough again to make us happy. And it happened with the same stuff that had made it happen in '69. It was magic pushing mortals over the line. It was crazy fans, and signs, and good players who could hypnotize themselves into greatness. Nineteen seventy-three was beautiful. But we would never have this team again. We would never have another September or October of 1973. Supreme folly would now join with fate to destroy what remained of 1969. What was left would be ripped up like the grass on our field after we beat the Reds. That was exuberance. This was vandalism: the loss of Staub, of McGraw, of Seaver, of Kingman, of Matlack, and finally Koosman. We were left with nothing. But we would always have '73. The Miracle of '69 had one last flicker of beautiful life, because we believed.

Rusty Staub

There has never been a ballplayer like Rusty Staub. An athlete and a chef, he looked more like a chef. And he ran the bases like a chef. But he was an astonishing right fielder with a powerful arm. It didn't make sense that someone so slow could play the outfield so well. He demonstrated the way in which a lot of intelligence and heart and some kind of mysterious perfect alignment of eye and nerves can make up for physical deficiencies. Rusty's hitting and fielding helped to bring us a pennant in 1973. He got us to the playoffs and then he stopped the charge of the great Reds team with a historic catch in the fourth game of the playoffs. If he hadn't hurt himself making that catch, smashing into the right field wall, the Mets might have done to the A's what they did to the Reds.

Rusty was a fine hitter, one of the best clutch hitters ever. His hitting epitomized the '73 team. He was classy and good, but he was hardly overwhelming. Still, with just a very good average and home run total, he drove in lots of runs. Like the '73 team, he got as far as he did by coming through just at the right moments. Then, at the end of his best season, 1975, in one of those mind-boggling trades that Met fans believe only the Mets make, Rusty was traded at the peak of his powers to Detroit for Mickey Lolich, a pitcher who was the same shape as Rusty, but was at a different point in his career. Lolich bombed. Rusty thrived. And then, years later, when his own skills finally began to wane, Rusty came back to the Mets.

He came back as a designated hitter, which we couldn't really use, of course. There was no reason why this big, slow man, who could still hit but could no longer do anything else, should have been playing in the National League in his late thirties. But the fact that he came back seemed to suggest that he still loved us, and he still loved our city, where he could feel at home and where he owned a restaurant.

In the early eighties, we were able to enjoy Rusty as a consummate hitting artist and technician. He hit over .400 as a pinch hitter, and set a record with eight consecutive pinch hits. It was a lot of fun to arrive at the moment in the game when Rusty was unwrapped and brought to the plate. Always a showman, Rusty made these moments count with his careful manner, and his hitting rituals. Focused and meticulous, he treated his bats and his shoes and his batting gloves as a chef treats his knives. He implied that hitting was as much of an art and a science as cooking. You had to have the right implements, the right training, the right instincts, and you had to be sure to clean up after yourself. The rituals were part of Rusty's mystique, and I'm sure they were intended to psych out the pitchers. They worked. Everyone believed that this uncharacteristically stout and elegant man had discovered some special techniques, some special secrets of hitting.

Rusty had poise and a baby-like handsomeness. The toast of Montreal, he was immediately welcomed and loved by cosmopolitan New York. He is the only player I have ever seen about whom it could be said that he played with aplomb. He was graceful and stylish, a confirmed bachelor as they used to say, with no rumored girlfriends past or present. It seemed likely to many that Rusty was gay. But to my retrospective amazement, no one ever went near that. I don't even remember hearing any crap from assholes in the stands. Because he was so good, Rusty was allowed his unfamiliar uniqueness. Protected by his bat, his philanthropy, and his friendly, intelligent, manly polish, Rusty's difference from other ballplayers seemed analogous to his vividly different natural hair color. The Quebecois had called him "Le Grand Orange" and we kept it up. Bright orange is the hair color of eccentrics. I suppose that many may have thought that the hair was ultimately the reason why this guy didn't come across in the same way as the unelegant ballplayers with ordinary hair colors. Or maybe it was because he came from New Orleans, a strange and colorful place that produces so many unusual gifted people.

I don't know if Rusty is gay, but I'd like to think he is. I'm sick and tired of the pretense that no ballplayer is gay. Everyone knows that there is no reason why gays can't be fine ballplayers. Everyone knows that there are gay ballplayers. Sure some jerks will shout stuff, as they shouted stuff at Jackie Robinson. But they stopped with Robinson, didn't they? Rusty would be a perfect person to break this stupid barrier, because he was very popular, he is no longer playing, and he has already done his bit to stretch our idea of what a ballplayer is supposed to be like. If he is gay, though, I can hardly blame him for not coming out. He has a good life. Why should he have to sacrifice his privacy? He has already given us a great deal. Why should he be expected to take on something so much more difficult than being the greatest pinch hitter who ever lived?

Eddie Kranepool

What kind of memories do I have of Eddie Kranepool? What kind of memories do you have of Eddie Kranepool? All of us over a certain age have a sense that Eddie Kranepool is as much a part of the history of the franchise as Mr. Met. He was a Met for 18 years, far longer than anyone else. Memories of Eddie Kranepool must be an important part of being a Mets fan. What do you remember? We loved Eddie Kranepool. Why? It wasn't because he was good. It wasn't because he was nice or interesting. It was because he was a kind of tradition. Okay. What kind of tradition?

Well, he played for us in the very first year of the team, at the age of 17. He didn't play much, about two games I think, but it seems to me that you would hear about him as an important part of the Mets' future. I'm not sure why they thought this. In retrospect it seems very hard to imagine that anyone could ever have looked at Eddie Kranepool and thought that he would hit .300 or hit 40 home runs or anything. But maybe that's just because we know what happened. Or what didn't happen.

Eddie didn't happen. But he didn't exactly not happen either. He played well enough to survive in the major leagues for 18 years, but he never had a successful season as a full-fledged regular on the team. That's pretty amazing when you think about it. He was a regular for a while. He had success after a while. It's just that the two things didn't happen at the same time, as you might have expected them to.

Eddie didn't do anything like he was supposed to. He was like a grouchy toy robot that a kid can't get to operate correctly. Eddie wasn't handsome, but you had a sense that he was supposed to be. That is to say that he had black hair and a square head and a square jaw. He was close enough to that 1960s Superman look. He had a nice sort of chucklehead smile, but he reserved it for when he was being photographed, with a bat. He looked more at ease on a baseball card than on the field.

So the Yankees had Mickey Mantle and Roger Maris and we had Eddie Kranepool. How come theirs worked and ours didn't? The one we got even had a weird name.

But like the stubborn kid who has gotten shortchanged, we preferred the one we ended up with. We hugged him and encouraged him. We cheered his meager triumphs. He was ours. He'd hit .250, with numbing regularity, and he'd normally break into the double digits for home runs. Surly as he was, he expected our approval when he did his great deeds. We gave it up for him.

Eventually we got the other one too, the one who was equally funny-named and disappointing. They were our two sluggers, our two bright hopes for the future. Kranepool and Swoboda. Now if we could only get some pitching.

When the pitching came and Hodges came, Eddie and Ron got to be part of the real big story. It's always a surprise to realize that they were still around when the Mets got good. You want even more of a surprise? Eddie was still around when the Mets got bad again. He was like the thing that wouldn't leave. He was like the Wandering Jew. He had several lifetimes, none of them entirely satisfying. Everyone else would come and go. Not Eddie. Nobody ever talked about trading him. It was like he wasn't an actual player who could play on another team. He was just part of the Mets.

Eddie got better after we had given up on him. After he stayed stuck through the sixties and was sent down to the minors, and eventually was resurrected as the less interesting half of a platoon, he got better. At least his statistics improved. But that may have been because he didn't have to hit all kinds of pitching. He never became a power hitter. He was an okay first baseman. One year he hit .280 and then there was a year when after all the smoke cleared, there was a .323 next to his name and no one could figure out how it got there.

Eddie at the end became a distinguished pinch hitter. It was great when he came to the plate, and we could shout "Ed-die! Ed-die!" As the clouds darkened as the seventies waned, it livened things up towards the end of a game.

Eddie was more the Mets than anyone else. He was a beloved disappointment. An incompetent who became indispensable. He wasn't good, but he was filled with surprises. And after you got used to the fact that he wouldn't do anything much, you would see him come to the plate, and you would cheer him and then he would stroke a beautiful single into right and win the ball game for you.

1977–1982

Fans who followed the Mets closely from 1977 to 1982 share a special bond. We don't, in any conventional sense, have wonderful memories to share. Not only do we not have a division title, pennant, or championship to remember, we cannot even remember a period in which we were in contention, for even a few minutes. The Mets did not get close to .500 during these seven years, except for a few seconds of artificial excitement during a fresh start in the second half of the strike-split season of 1981. And looking back, there was never any legitimate reason to think that we would contend, or even get close to .500. The Mets had been just as bad during their first seven seasons, but it made all kinds of sense to root for them in the beginning.

It made no sense at all to root for the Mets from 1977 to 1982. The Mets were not new. They had a history. They had reached an improbable pinnacle, winning a world championship and two pennants. And then they were destroyed by the stubborn reactionary greed and stupidity of the fool, M. Donald Grant, who ran the team for Mrs. Payson's clueless daughter and granddaughters. The daughter and granddaughters had the kind of names a rich girl might have given to her dolls. I can remember sitting in the nearly empty stadium as the granddaughters proudly rode from home plate to the bullpen in a carriage drawn by a favorite horse that they hoped would win the hearts of the fans as a new mascot. It was such an embarrassing moment that I felt sorry for them. Having inherited their grandmother's toy, they did not seem to understand the role it played in the lives of the rest of us. They wanted us to be happy, but they had no clue about how to make us happy. And they and their mother were only doing what their grandmother's financial advisor was telling them to do.

While Grant ran that team, the Mets as a business did not deserve our patronage. And looking back, I cannot remember how I convinced myself to continue to give it. How well I remember the horrible evening of June 15, 1977. I remember Dave Kingman, our only exciting hitter, given away in the night. I remember Tom Seaver, the greatest Met ever, traded to Cincinnati for four prospects. I am amazed that this could have happened, that this could have been done to millions of fans, when so little money was at stake. But what amazes me most about that evening is what I did the next morning. I looked carefully over the statistics of the four prospects who had been traded for Seaver, and I worked myself into a frenzy of hope and excitement.

I was a dupe. But it was not M. Donald Grant who duped me. I did it to myself. I found it hard to give up Seaver. But I found it impossible to give up my hopes and dreams about the Mets. And so a cycle began that lasted through the seven years of drought. It began with the rosy dreaming that June morning of the marvelous future promised by Pat Zachry and Steve Henderson. I remember how, at the end of that year, I compared Steve Henderson's rookie totals with Jackie Robinson's and found that they were pretty close. Surely it was inevitable that someone who hit .297 in his rookie year would hit .342 by his third year, as Robinson did? Pat Zachry had been a Rookie of the Year, and then somewhere in there I think we also got Butch Metzger, who had also been a Rookie of the Year.

There were, it seemed to me, a lot of things to get excited about. I thought Doug Flynn had to be the best defensive second baseman ever and I was very proud of him. John Stearns, tough and scrappy and all that, could have been the catcher on any contending team. Lee Mazilli was pretty good, although he never became as good as he was scripted to be, just as he was never quite as handsome as he was supposed to be. Joel Youngblood seemed to be an exciting ballplayer and one year, remember, Craig Swan won the ERA title. The minors seemed rich and promising. The team was sold to Doubleday and Wilpon and so you could legitimately say that we were rebuilding. One year it looked as if we could even dream of contending if Swan, Zachry, Espinosa, and Falcone, our first halfway-decent starting rotation in a long time, could only stay healthy.

What we needed was that eternally elusive (for the Mets) missing piece: the real threat in the middle of line-up. And so, the new owners began to invest in a series of the kind of players the Mets have always gotten, the established players, the sure bets, who ride into Shea and turn into pumpkins. In that era, there was Willie Montanez, Richie Hebner, and Eliott Maddux. They came and they went. And they didn't stop you from building up your hopes about the next established player who would succumb to Shea's unfathomable reverse alchemy.

Year after year, the team would begin with hope and then unravel. My hopes would not just be dashed. They'd be mocked and ripped to shreds. You'd give up the dream of contention, and then the dream of respectability. You'd reach the point where you could be satisfied with just a few gleams and glitters. An unexpected victory here, a good defensive play there, a sign of improvement that might continue into next year. In the end, none of the players who stirred my imagination were good enough to carry the team anywhere. I learned in those years what any astute baseball fan must know: that bad teams have a lot of good players. They just don't have enough great ones. I also learned something about the deepest mystery of baseball fandom. Without any realistic hope, deep into seasons in which first place is more than 30 games away, it is still possible to have fun.

The stadium was spacious and friendly in those years. I'd buy my General Admission ticket, sit upstairs for the first inning, and then go down and find a great seat in the Loge for the rest of the game. Nobody bothered me or asked to see my ticket. The crowds were small but very enthusiastic. We couldn't make the deafening roar of the recent past, but you could actually hear individual people cheering, excited people, involved people. And of course, the only people who came were the purest Met fans you could find. No one was indifferent. No one was there because the Yankees weren't as good. Everyone was as much of a needy fool as I was. We were the crazy ones. And we felt we were holding the fort till the rest of the crowd came back. For this, we felt, we should be thanked and praised and remembered in glory. We had earned the right to feel the contempt we knew we would feel when the rest of them came back and pretended that they hadn't been gone.

To this day, I smile inside when I talk to lifelong Met fans who don't know who Frank Taveras was. These fans know all about Al Weis and Ed Charles, and they say they remember Hubie Brooks and Mookie Wilson shaking things up in the early eighties. But they were not in the trenches with us, as we dreamed about Dan Norman's power swing or Juan Berenguer's 100 mph fastball. I don't blame them. But after twenty-five years, I allow myself the indulgence of pitying them.

Meeting a Met

Only once in my life have I ever met a Met. It wasn't the usual fan encounter. The Met did not sign my program and say two words to me that I would remember all my life. I spent a couple of hours with him, and a few other people. I did not ask for an autograph. Something within me could not bring myself to ask that of him. It wasn't an insignificant Met either. It was Tom Seaver. I was in his house in Greenwich, Connecticut. Nancy Seaver gave me lunch.

This was one of the strangest experiences of my life, and since I did not share it with anyone other than a few people I had never seen before and never saw again, there are even times when I do not feel that it actually happened. My antique dealer father-in-law had sold some eighteenth-century chairs to a friend of his, an antique dealer who was selling the chairs to a Cincinnati antiques dealer who was somehow involved in the marketing of a limited edition of casts of a sculpture of Seaver pitching. The Cincinnati antique dealer was visiting Seaver for some reason connected to the sculpture and he had gotten Seaver's permission to have my father-in-law's friend drop off the chairs at Seaver's house in Greenwich. My father-in-law's friend brought along his two sons, aspiring pitchers, now antique dealers. And in an act of generosity that embarrassed and amazed me, he offered to have me accompany them, since he knew I was a Mets fan. I had a token usefulness. I carried two chairs from one van to another. For this service, or rather because of this extraordinary accident, I was entertained in the home of my greatest baseball hero.

At first, I didn't want to do it. When my father-in-law called me in the morning to ask if I wanted to go to Tom Seaver's house, I told him that I couldn't. I was under a lot of pressure at the time, working on my dissertation. I really was under a lot of pressure. I wasn't taking any breaks. The final copy of my dissertation had to be delivered in just a couple of weeks. I tried to hide behind this. I was trying to insist that some things were real and some things were not. I would not abandon my sense of my real life for what promised to be the rarest of all possible glimpses of something beyond real life. Then I stared into space for about three minutes, hearing a voice I have only heard a few times, a voice inside of me that belongs to my life, as a whole thing, as something somewhat separate from me. My life told me that I had to do this, whether I was comfortable with it or not, because the important thing was not whether I was comfortable but whether my life was going to be as memorable and as amazing as it could possibly be. I called my father-in-law back. I told him I would go. He had been hurt by my original decision. He didn't understand what I was feeling. Now, he was happy. His friend picked me up a few hours later. We drove to Greenwich.

I always knew that Seaver lived in Greenwich, but of course people don't actually know where in a town celebrities live. The neighbors know, but they keep such things as secret as they can be kept. As we turned off the Merritt Parkway at an exit I had passed many times, I made a point of not remembering how we drove to his house. It seemed to me to be unfair that a stranger was now going to learn exactly where he lived. Wasn't it bad for strangers to know where you lived if you were just trying to live your life and millions of people wanted to know where you lived?

I do remember that it was a big modern house. Inside, the vast modern spaces were filled with a beautiful collection of American antiques. The house was solid, friendly, capacious, and because of the antiques, somewhat cultivated. It looked like Seaver's house. When we got there, we were welcomed by Nancy, and we were told that Tom was throwing in the basement. We were offered seats at a big dining room table. On the wall facing me were three magnificent grandfather clocks and three Cy Young awards. I'm not fricking kidding.

We heard sounds in the cellar and people coming up the stairs. There were a couple of men associated with the marketing of this sculpture and there, in workout clothes, was Seaver. Since he wasn't rail thin, and because he had that big head and almost babyish face, I had always thought of Seaver as a little chunky. He wasn't. In his sweat pants, his legs looked like the thickest, strongest things I had ever seen.

He saw us and was immediately in host mode. He had the friendly smoothness of a career diplomat. This is how he treated my father-in-law's friend, a funny-looking antique dealer who really had no real right to be there, his two silent adolescent sons, and me, a large, bearded graduate student, who was at several removes from having a right to be there. He knew that all we could really have wanted was the right to see him and hear him. We had nothing to give him. I was so embarrassed by this. I thought for a moment that I might be able to offer him something by saying that I was such a great Mets fan and he had always been my favorite player and I remember all his greatest moments. But I felt that that was what everyone said to him. Maybe it meant something to him every time he heard it, maybe it didn't. I didn't know. I didn't know what to do. I wished I could disappear, but I still wanted to be there. He excused himself to shower and change.

Nancy laid out some cold cuts and things for a snack-lunch in this big kitchen next to the dining room. In the morning the Seavers, we were told, had gone to Rockefeller Center to see the Christmas show. I looked at one of Seaver's daughters, a little girl with golden hair, and I thought of how she had had to come back home so her father could attend to what must have been, for a little girl, this dreary business matter. This was the reason the family, that could be together only part of the year, couldn't have walked down Fifth Avenue to see the window displays, couldn't have gone to F.A.O. Schwarz and to Rumpelmayer's. These big silent men, several of whom had just come to be in the presence of her father. She looked up at her mother and said, "I guess we have company." I guess they did.

But when Seaver came back from his shower, he didn't seem to think that there was anything wrong with us being there. He kindly gave us his time. He talked with us about baseball. He acted like we were friends of his. He even explained, with fairness, and without any false humility, why he and not Fernando Valenzuela had deserved the Cy Young Award for the past season (1981). As it happened, I agreed with him. I could explain why he deserved it and not Valenzuela. But he already knew the reasons and I didn't say anything. I gave him a lot of credit for not pretending to feel that the younger pitcher deserved it, just so that he could have come across as modest and humble. He knew that he deserved his fourth Cy Young and he knew it wasn't fair that he hadn't gotten it.

Before we left, Seaver took us into a little study that held his own private collection of memorabilia. There was a barrel with baseballs marked with all of the major moments of his career.

What right had I to see that barrel of sacred baseballs? What right had I to see those Cy Young awards? What right had I to eat the man's food? What right had I to see the golden hair of his little daughters? What right had I to see his legs like tree trunks across a dining room, not in a uniform, not from two hundred feet away? No right.

He shook all our hands as we left. I had not said a word all afternoon. I had had many things to say, but I felt that my presence was enough of a burden, was enough of a violation. He didn't need to have to hear my voice as well, or my baseball opinions, or my love and my gratitude. I really don't think Seaver saw it that way. If he knew what was happening in my head, he would have told me to relax. He would have said he was glad to see me. But I could not have thought this. I felt that

I was not worthy of what was happening to me. His hand was strong. In the moment of that handshake I just let it happen and I felt everything in that moment of contact. I said the only words I would say all afternoon. I said "Thank you."

1984

In 1984, the Mets had a new slogan: "Catch the Rising Stars." The words were put up on the stadium and the Mets TV station, Channel 9, had what I thought was an adorable jingle that went along with it. I don't remember the exact words and I won't take the trouble to find the exact words because what you remember, which in my case is probably all I ever knew, is what a jingle really is: "There's a little bit of something in everyone. There's the joy of sharing a dream. There's a little bit of something in everyone. Being part of the team. Catch the rising stars. Catch the rising stars. The Mets are all the world to see. The Mets are all for you and me-ee. Catch the rising stars. Catch the rising stars. Watch them here on Channel 9." Obviously all remotely competent slogans are of equal quality. What makes them good or bad is what happens while they're being used. "Ya Gotta Believe" would have seemed cruel and disgusting in 1977. "Catch the Rising Stars" would have made you retch in 1993. But "Catch the Rising Stars," and its associated TV jingle were, it turns out, just right for 1984.

It was right because it had the Mets corniness and sentimentality. It had the spirit of "Meet the Mets" as it would translate into the soulful sincere style of a seventies–eighties jingle ("We spend our days like bright and shiny new dimes…"). We were being asked to catch a falling star and put it in our pocket so that it might never fade away. The fifth-grade chorus has always urged us to do this at the spring assembly. But this time, we were going to catch a "rising" rather than a falling star, because that's what they call young and talented ballplayers. Perfect. You put this slogan up on a stadium and you cross your fingers.

1984

No one was prepared for what would rise up out of the sorry ruins of those seven lost years. Sure we had more hope at the start of the '84 season, because we had gotten Keith Hernandez, for some reason we couldn't understand. Great players didn't just come to the Mets. Only bad players came to the Mets, in trades for people who would later become great players. If someone who was supposed to be great came to the Mets, they would wilt right in front of our eyes. Hernandez was a mystery. He wasn't wilting and we got him for nothing. And we'd have a whole year of Strawberry, who had won the Rookie-of-the-Year award and should just get better. So we felt at the start of the '84 season that maybe we had a shot at respectability. No one expected more.

We got more. And it was beautiful. And it was as close as the Mets have ever gotten to a repeat of 1969. As in 1969, there really were rising stars. And their gleam was steady and not just in our eyes. Dwight Gooden was not Pat Zachry. Ron Darling was not Pete Falcone. And Darryl Strawberry was certainly not Lee Mazzilli.

But we weren't fated to win this time. It looked as if we might as Frank Cashen and Davey Johnson built the team around decent offense at every position and surprisingly solid starting pitching, with two rookies at the top of the rotation. Johnson was amazingly intelligent and he was respected by his players. He also had, along with Cashen, a kind of Orioles mystique about him. Even though we had beaten them in 1969, Mets fans had the sense that the Orioles knew the right way to do things. The Mets would sometimes win, but they never knew what they were doing, which was why they couldn't build a dynasty or even repeat success two years in a row. The Orioles used computers, they treated the game like a science, they flew in the face of orthodoxies that could be mathematically disproven. And they knew exactly when to turn off the computer and start flying manually. Davey Johnson would manage like Earl Weaver and we had no complaints.

But if one irony of the 1984 season is that Orioles methods got us as far as they did, the other irony was that the Cubs beat us. The Cubs had a little more talent and a lot more experience than we had. When the Mets wavered in August, the Cubs took advantage and built a lead we would not overcome. We could see, though, that their dominance wouldn't last. The Cubs were generally in their thirties. Some of them looked as if they might even have been around in 1969. The Mets were new. They had almost enough offense and they had a 19-year-old pitcher who, in September, pitched as no pitcher, rookie or veteran, had ever pitched before.

Dwight Gooden

In the forty-five years I have been a baseball fan, the five best pitchers have been, in my opinion: Sandy Koufax, Tom Seaver (I hate to admit it but...), Roger Clemens, Randy Johnson, and Pedro Martinez. I offer an honorable mention to Juan Marichal, Bob Gibson, Jim Palmer, and Greg Maddux.

Sandy Koufax's three greatest seasons were 1963, when he was 25–5, with a 1.88 E.R.A. and 306 strikeouts in 311 innings; 1965, when he was 26–8, with a 2.04 E.R.A. and 382 strikeouts in 336 innings; and 1966, when he was 27–9, with a 1.73 E.R.A. and 317 strikeouts in 323 innings.

Tom Seaver's best years were 1969, when he was 25–7, with a 2.21 E.R.A. and 208 strikeouts in 273 innings; 1971, when he was 20–10, with a 1.76 E.R.A. and 289 strikeouts in 286 innings; and 1975, when he was 22–9, with an E.R.A. of 2.38 and 243 strikeouts in 280 innings.

Roger Clemens's best years were 1986, when he was 24–4, with a 2.48 E.R.A. with 238 strikeouts in 254 innings; 1990, when he was 21–6, with an E.R.A. of 1.93, with 209 strikeouts in 228 innings; and 1997, when he was 21–7, with a 2.05 E.R.A. and 292 strikeouts in 264 innings.

Pedro Martinez's best years were 1999, when he had a record of 23–4, an E.R.A. of 2.07 and 313 strikeouts in 213 innings; 2000, when he had a record of 18–6, an E.R.A. of 1.74, and 284 strikeouts in 217 innings; and 2002, when he had a record of 20–4, with a 2.26 E.R.A. and 239 strikeouts in 199 innings.

Randy Johnson best seasons were 1997, when he was 20–4, with a 2.28 E.R.A. and 291 strikeouts in 213 innings; 2001, when he was 21–6 with a 2.49 E.R.A. and 372 strikeouts in 249 innings; and 2002, when he was 24–5 with a 2.32 E.R.A. and 334 strikeouts in 260 innings.

In 1985, Dwight Gooden had a record of 24–4. His E.R.A. was 1.53 and he struck out 268 batters in 277 innings. If you compare this season to the best seasons of the best pitchers of the past 45 years, you will see that it is, if just barely, better than all the rest of them.

Gooden's unbelievable season of 1985 had a glorious penumbra. At the end of 1984, Gooden won eight of his last nine starts. Over those nine games, he had an E.R.A. of 1.05. In April of 1986, Gooden was 4–0, with a 1.26 E.R.A. If you add these totals to the 1985 season, Gooden had a span of 41 decisions during which he was 36–5, with an E.R.A. between 1.3 and 1.4, striking out something like 400 batters. I don't know of any evidence that any pitcher has ever done anything comparable at any point in his career.

When Koufax had his greatest seasons, he was 27, 29, and 30. When Seaver had his greatest seasons, he was 24, 26, and 30. When Clemens had his greatest seasons, he was 24, 28, and 35. Martinez was 28, 29, and 31. Johnson was 34, 38, and 39.

In 1985, Dwight Gooden was 20 years old.

Only a handful of pitchers were ever nearly as good as Gooden was when Gooden was 20. And none of these pitchers was even remotely this good at the age of 20. The only one of these pitchers who pitched in the major leagues when he was 20 was Koufax, who, in 1955, was 2–2, with a 3.02 E.R.A., and 30 strikeouts in 41 innings.

I will say it. Here it is.

Dwight Gooden had more talent than any pitcher in the modern era of baseball.

Baseball is not about numbers. But baseball is often about the sublime, the beautiful terror of magnitude. And the only language we have for this is numbers. One of the greatest pleasures I have had as a Mets fan was seeing Gooden when he was 19 and 20. I remember the games behind these numbers. I remember him striking out the side in his first All-Star game appearance. I remember him striking out 16 batters in two consecutive games. I remember how perfectly unhittable he was. I remember how excited I was. I remember what it felt like as these unprecedented numbers assumed their permanent form. I savored them, I thought of them over and over. I couldn't believe that I was alive to see this. I couldn't believe that this was being done by a Met.

Other Mets have come close to giving me something like this. Seaver and Piazza are among the all-time greats and they had some of their all-time great seasons with the Mets. Strawberry looked as if someday he would have a Ted Williams or Babe Ruth season. But he never did. Gooden, however, did have this season that put him in a clubhouse with Lefty Grove, Dizzy Dean, Cy Young, and Grover Cleveland Alexander. And his youth and poise and his beautiful motion offered the promise of many more seasons of solid gold.

Gooden, in the moment he stepped from the heavens, was sublime. There has never been a pitcher like him. And few of us are likely to see a talent of his magnitude again.

1985

Just as we didn't win in 1984, we didn't win in 1985. We didn't win even though Gooden pitched what might have been the best pitcher's season of the modern era. We didn't win even though we had terrific new players like Roger McDowell, Sid Fernandez, and Lenny Dykstra. We didn't win even though Keith Hernandez, Ron Darling, and Gary Carter all had wonderful seasons for us. Strawberry's spectacular second half, the Curley Shuffle, and all of the wonderful feelings in the happy, noisy stadium were not quite enough. The dark years were gone, just like that. It was now a good time, and it felt as if the good times would last at least as long as the bad time that had just ended. The Mets were a better team in 1985 than they had been in 1984. Though they were young, they were good enough to win the pennant. But the Cardinals were a little better.

We were neck and neck with the Cardinals all season, usually just a little bit behind. Somehow, I figured, we would pass them in the last few weeks, pass them with our youth, our talent, our hype, and our enthusiasm. It almost happened. We took two out of three from the Cards and went into first on September 12, but then we fell back again. We needed a three-game sweep to tie the Cardinals when we faced them in the second-to-last series of the season. But we won only two. Then we lost two of three to the Expos and the Cardinals took what was theirs.

So it didn't happen. Maybe it was because the Mets were so young and so talented that they felt that they had all the time in the world. Maybe 1984 and 1985 together should remind us that we never have all the time in the world.

The defining moment of 1985 was that famous last game at Shea, the game in which the crowd went wild when they saw the highlights of the season on the Diamond Vision, and the players, overcome with emotion, threw their hats into the stands. All Mets fans remember this, whether they were there or not, whether they watched this or not. This moment stood for us at our best. It defined Mets love: the sweet, spontaneous, loud, and tender friendship of our fans and our players. Whether we win or not, this is what matters to us the most: these moments when we all just relax and cheer and feel grateful for what we have. At moments like this, we see how we are a community, how we share a history and a tradition. We share something that we have all made room for in our lives. All Mets fans felt this way when we saw or heard what happened at that last game of the 1985 season. We didn't win the division. But we had this great big moment of knowing that we were Mets fans and we had the Mets.

Nineteen eighty-four and 1985 felt wonderful while they were happening. But in the collective memory of Mets fans, these two seasons have receded. Their greatest moments are rarely remembered. Now they are thought of as the opening act, as the first course, as chopped liver.

Nineteen eighty-six was so bright that everything around it is dim.

1986: The Bad Guys Won?

Nowadays when you hear about the 1986 Mets, you hear that they were brash and cocky and scrappy and badly behaved. They liked to drink and party together. I guess they made a mess on a plane once or something. And players on other teams are supposed to have hated their New York swagger and so they threw baseballs at their heads and that led to fights and so you get the adjective "brawling" to go with all the others.

I have to be honest. I don't remember 1986 like this at all. Sure, I knew about the beanballs and the fights. But I hated it when other teams threw at the Mets because of the stupid rule that baseball players are supposed to keep a lid on their exuberance. The 1986 Mets were exuberant. They had reason to be. The Mets were so far in front that they had to play like that in order to stay involved. I resented other teams for resenting this so much.

Maybe they were brash. I've read that players on other teams didn't like Gary Carter. I loved the way Carter played. I loved his open-faced, puppy dog pleasure in how good he was. But I could see how this could get on people's nerves. Dykstra was brash. He had the whole "Nails" thing, the Pete Rose thing, which, frankly, turned me off at the time. Looking back on it, I can appreciate it. But in 1986, I was such a fan of Mookie Wilson, and therefore so afraid of Dykstra taking his job, that I could not get into the "Nails" thing. Dykstra was very very good. And he was brash.

Fans enjoy the hype they like and they ignore the hype they don't like. In this way, fans make their own team, just as they make their own salad at the salad bar. The brash, brawling, boozer, and bruiser stuff wasn't on my screen, just as onions aren't in my salad.

What I remember about the 1986 Mets is that they were so unbelievably good.

They were insanely good. I had never seen a better baseball team. As a Mets fan I found it hard to get used to the idea that the Mets were actually this good. The 1969 team had been unexpectedly good. The 1973 team managed to win a pennant and almost win a World Series without even being particularly good. But the 1986 team was great. They were in a class with the 1927 Yankees and the 1975 Reds. They won 108 games. They won almost as many games as the 1962 Mets lost.

They didn't lack anything. They had five first-rate starting pitchers. What more do you need? You don't need anything more. But they had more. Dykstra and Backman, the twin midget wrestlers at the top of the order, would get on base, and then there were five guys who could drive them in. There was always enough offense. If the 1986 Mets had ever fallen behind, they would always have been able to come back.

They hummed. After they got on top, no one came anywhere near them. They played well at home and they played well on the road. They played well at the beginning of the season, in the middle, and at the end. The pitching was great, the hitting was great, the defense was great. They were a feast of competence and consistency. The baseball universe was in a once-in-a-lifetime harmony. You just heard music.

And they looked so good. I guess a team that looked like these guys could have won 60 games instead of 108. But it doesn't seem possible. It's not that they were all handsome. They didn't blend into a mass of big chests and broad smiles. It's more that each one of them looked like himself. Each player was completely distinct. Most of them were, in fact, unusual. But each of them looked like a winner in a way that you wouldn't expect. I know I'm not making sense, but this is the impression they created. Yet even though they were all so unique and so individual, they also came in clumps and in contrasting pairs.

There was Gooden and there was Strawberry (oh the tears and despair to think of it). They were so young and so movingly gifted. They were both tall, handsome men with the faces of boys. Gooden and Strawberry seemed so young but they had none of the transparency of youth. You watched them at rest and you couldn't tell if they were calm or melancholy. You watched them fidget and you couldn't tell if they were excited or restless. Who knows what they were? Who knows what they were thinking?

It meant a lot to me that Mookie was still on the '86 team. I loved how Mookie played. I loved how fast he was, how sweet and kind and good he seemed. I loved the feeling of his delight in his play, and I loved how it felt so different from Dykstra's as they fought for their jobs all summer. I was sad that Mookie spent so much of the season injured or on the bench. I was so happy that the most important moment of 1986 restored him to the prominence I wanted for him.

Keith Hernandez was the center of the club. You could tell why everyone followed him, and not anyone else. He looked like he knew what he was doing, as he stroked his line drives, as he kept the infield and the pitcher focused, as he played first base as no one had ever played it, as if it was a position that required intelligence and total alertness and perfect reflexes. But Keith's magnificence was not a sunny thing. It seemed haunted, somber, and intense. And this affected how you looked at Gary Carter. You were relieved and slightly put off by Gary's happy hustle. Carter was the greater athlete. He, and not Keith, is in the Hall of Fame. Carter could do a lot and was proud of what he could do. Keith looked as if he had been pressed into action. He looked as if he had to give something up to be this good. He had to concentrate very hard. He had none of Carter's uncomplicated delight. He looked as if he was afraid that if he didn't hold things together, everything would spin out of control.

Our pitching staff didn't look like anybody else's pitching staff. Pitchers are often awkward and geeky. Not these guys. Each of them had his own version of pitcher's cool. Gooden took your breath away, as a 21-year-old Hall-of-Famer. But on this pitching staff, he was far from the whole story. Darling was so unique, he seemed almost fictional, with his name, his Yalie self-possession, and his exotic, handsome face. Ojeda came across as a deeply ironic suburban dad while Sid Fernandez was thick and fire-breathing. The pair of closers, McDowell and Orosco, were like an act. Each was a laid back guy from California, but one looked like a cowboy and the other looked like an Indian. They finished each and every game like masters of their craft and then fooled around in the dugout like a pair of clowns.

The '86 team also had its wild cards: imperfect and inconsistent players with either too much or too little hair and maybe too much personality. You couldn't ever know how much Ray Knight had left, or whether

Hojo or Kevin Mitchell would ever amount to anything. These three guys were funny-looking and wacko and they were alternately brilliant and awful. But they were the guys in the boiler room. They kept things moving, and they came through when you didn't expect it. They were part of the flawless team, but they did a lot to keep it from feeling flawless.

Boy did I love the 1986 Mets. I loved how they were a great show, without ever being Hollywood. I loved how their concentration never wavered, and how they stuck by each other. I loved how they stayed in the groove and never let up. I loved how after one of the best seasons by any team ever, they almost lost the playoffs, but didn't. I loved how they came close to losing the World Series, but didn't. I loved the way that teetering on the brink of failure made them feel more like a Mets team, like improbable heroes, when in fact there was nothing improbable about anything they achieved. I doubt I will ever see a Mets team as good as this. I'm sure I'll never see a Mets team that looks as good as this. They weren't the "bad guys" who won. They were good guys. And they won because they were so good, even if they almost lost because, however good they were, they were still the Mets.

The Most Exciting Mets Game Ever

When you are a fan of the best team in baseball, the playoffs and the World Series aren't always fun. You aren't cheering for your scrappy guys as they try to upset the lords of baseball. You are afraid that an undeserving team will deprive you of the championship you have earned.

The 1986 National League Championship Series against the Astros wasn't fun for Mets fans. We were a better team, but they had Mike Scott. Scott had pitched for us, during the terrible early eighties, and when he did, he wasn't very good. But somewhere he had learned this incredible pitch, what was supposed to be a split-fingered fastball. It did things that no pitch had ever done before. It acted like there was somebody inside of it. The Mets were convinced that Scott was cheating, that he was scuffing the ball. But you could tell that they weren't completely sure. They also didn't want to look as if they were crybabies. We were fans, we didn't know.

You realize at moments like this that however much you love the Mets, you don't know them. I was a fan but I was not such an idiot as to believe that Scott was cheating just because the Mets said he was. I've also never been entirely sure that Cleon Jones was actually hit in the foot by the ball that had shoe polish on it. Maybe that was Cleon's ball and maybe it wasn't. Maybe Scott was cheating. Whatever he was doing, he was going to win, because the Mets were completely psyched out.

Scott won the first game. The Mets won the next two. Scott won the fourth game. Then the Mets won the fifth game. Going into the sixth game with a 3–2 edge, you'd think that the Mets would feel good about their chances. They didn't. Everybody knew that if the Astros won game six, Scott would win game seven.

The game was played on a weekday afternoon. Somehow my father and I and my two sisters were able to take time off from work. We gathered at my parents' home to see the game. We didn't do this kind of thing very often, even on a weekend. But we knew that we wanted to see this game together. We wanted the Mets either to win the pennant, or go down, in the very room where the Mets had won the '69 Series, the room where Neil Armstrong stepped onto the moon, where Jack Ruby shot Lee Harvey Oswald, and where Santa Claus once left us presents. This was the room, the center of our family life. Every family has a room like this. We called it the "den." It wasn't the largest or most impressive room in our house. It was pretty small. But it was where we had always spent most of our time. In New York and its suburbs, there were millions of rooms like this, and millions of families were gathering as we were.

If you could fly over New York and remove the roofs, you would see millions of versions of what you saw in our den. On the couch to the left as you face the TV, there was my mother and my thirty-year-old sister, Jennifer. On the two armchairs to the right were my father and my twenty-six-year-old sister, Stefanie. I, at thirty-two, was in a rocking chair in the center of the room. In back of me was the fireplace and around us were the paintings and clocks that had always been on the walls, and shelves and cabinets that held what my parents had bought in many different places because when you go someplace, you have to buy something.

The sixth game of the 1986 NLCS was not as much fun to experience as it is to remember. The Astros had jumped on Bobby Ojeda in the first inning, and they led 3–0 through all of the first eight. The Mets couldn't do anything against Bob Knepper, and even though Ojeda calmed down and Rick Aguilera pitched beautifully in relief, those three runs from the first inning could not come off the scoreboard. For eight innings, we were nervous and glum and we ate peanuts and tangerines. The other families ate whatever was their den food.

We were all together and we were watching the Mets. The game was so tense and important that we couldn't talk about our lives or about other things during the commercials. Nothing for those few hours was allowed to intrude. All of us cared, to an impossible depth, and all of us cared in different ways. I had once been the biggest Mets fan in the family, when I was the only little boy and it was the 1960s. But I hadn't been the most involved fan in my family for years. My sisters became much bigger fans than I was during the 1969 season and during the exciting seasons after that, as I was drifting away into whatever I did with my late adolescence. Their fandom was different from mine. It had less to do with the majesty and intricacy of numbers. It involved a more powerful embrace of the players themselves, of what they were as imaginary people.

In recent years, my parents had become more involved than any of us. They had more time. Now that we were grown, the Mets had taken part of our place. The Mets were the fourth kid, with their own share of all telephone conversations. The Mets now meant more to my parents than the Dodgers ever had. They watched every game here in the den, him in the bigger armchair to the right, her on the couch on the left. Nothing now changed in the den except that every year there were a few new things on the shelves.

Pinch-hitting for Aguillera, Lenny Dykstra led off the top of the ninth with a triple. Mookie singled him home. Kevin Mitchell grounded out and Mookie went to second. Then Keith Hernandez doubled and the score was 3–2, with Hernandez, the tying run, on second with one out. Knepper was finally finished. The new pitcher, Dave Smith, walked Gary Carter. Strawberry came to the plate and I dreamed of a long graceful home run to win the game. Strawberry hit one, but it was just foul. The Astros wouldn't take another chance. They pitched around Strawberry and he walked. So the tying run was on third with one out and Ray Knight hit a fly ball. The score was tied. But that was all we would get.

The next four innings were exquisite baseball hell. With everything in the balance, and the relief pitchers burning the furniture and then their arms and legs for fuel, no one could score a run. Then in the top of the fourteenth, the Mets gained the lead as Wally Backman drove in Darryl Strawberry. In the bottom of the fourteenth, Davey Johnson brought in the overused closer Jesse Orosco to replace Roger McDowell, who had pitched five perfect innings. Orosco struck out the first hitter, but then Billy Hatcher hit the kind of long slow-motion just-barely-not-foul home run that gets hit in the late innings of playoff games. The score was tied again. We were all back in the desperate limbo in which the inning began.

Nobody scored in the fifteenth. We wondered if the game could go on as long as the 24-inning, 1–0 game the Mets had lost to the Astros in 1968. This was already the longest postseason game in history.

People in Texas, I imagine, perhaps unjustly, were prayed out. We had eaten too much. We didn't want any more peanuts. We just wanted the game to be over. But if the game had to go on longer in order for the Mets to win, we would stay where we were. We would wait and we would watch and we would feel everything that happened. This is what fans do.

Strawberry led off the sixteenth. His funny little pop-up landed between the infielders and the center fielder. He ended up on second. Ray Knight singled him home. We were ahead again, but only by a run, and we had been there before. This lead was too fragile for this game. We needed more. Would we get more? The Astros made a pitching change. They brought in a lefty who threw a wild pitch that moved Knight to third. He walked Backman and then threw another wild pitch that scored Knight, as Backman went to second. Jesse Orosco bunted Backman to third. And Dykstra singled him home. We were ahead by three runs at the end of the inning.

Things looked good, but we remembered that Houston had been three runs ahead at the top of the ninth. And this game seemed to be happening in some kind of special strange space that no ordinary game ever entered. There was something in the game itself that was pushing the game to be more exciting, as exciting as it could possibly be. This was a dangerous force for us now. It had saved us before, but now we did not want any more excitement. Too bad. We got it.

Orosco, who normally pitched one inning and was now pitching his third, was tired, but the only pitchers left were the hapless Doug Sisk and the inexperienced Randy Niemann. You knew Johnson was right to put all his money on Jesse. He opened the inning striking out Reynolds. But then he walked Davey Lopes. Doran and then Hatcher hit singles off of Jesse's slower-than-usual fastball. Lopes scored but then Denny Walling hit into a fielder's choice. Glenn Davis came up, with two outs and runners on first and third. You didn't want this. Anything could have happened. Whatever happened would be historic and it could very easily be a disaster. My gut, perverse, told me that Davis would hit a home run. He didn't but he singled to center and the score was 6 to 5.

Jesse's fastball was gone, and there was still one more hitter, Kevin Bass, to get out. Jesse threw what he had left, sliders, in the way that in a horror movie people throw things at the monster to slow him down, because all they can do is throw things. Bass knew what to expect on every pitch but he couldn't connect. In what seemed like the longest, tensest at-bat in major league history, the count went full to 3–2. The crowd in Houston was screaming and not stopping for breath. Orosco pretended to peer into Carter for the sign. And then he threw one last perfect slider that broke perfectly over the middle of the plate. Bass swung, and hit nothing. Orosco threw his glove in the air, dropped to his knees, and was buried by the Mets.

Our den was not the right place for what happened next. My sisters and I leapt to our feet and began to do something we had never dreamed of doing as children, when we were much much smaller. We joined hands and began to jump up and down, and as the objects my parents had collected over the years did not begin to fall from their perches, we squeezed each others' hands and began to jump tentatively higher and higher, screaming because we were so happy that the Mets had won, that the Mets had survived, that they would not have to face Mike Scott. My parents are laughing and are pretending to be worried about the shelves and the cabinets toppling to the floor. I am filled with the joy I had at that moment, and the joy I feel looking back on us all there and complete and together.

Marrying the Red Sox

I didn't marry a Mets fan. My wife is from Massachusetts. She was a Red Sox fan, until October 25, 1986.

When I first met Sheila, in 1976, we enjoyed the fact that we were both such baseball fans. We joked about how lucky it was that although I was from New York, I was not a Yankee fan. Nobody ever thought of the Mets and the Red Sox as rivals. We were united by the intensity of our hatred of the Yankees. The Mets became Sheila's National League team and the Red Sox became my American League team. We loved our new teams in the way in which you can love your in-laws. The love was genuine, but it wasn't supposed to be the same thing as what you felt for your parents.

The Red Sox were a great team in the late seventies. The Mets stunk. When we were with my family, everyone was filled with love and hope for a team that could never win more than 70 games. When we were with her family, there was love for a team (Rice, Lynn, Fisk, Yaz, Evans, Scott, Tiant, etc.) that could not win fewer than 90 games. There was also hope, but it wasn't like any kind of hope I was familiar with. It wasn't a happy kind of hope. This puzzled me. Mets hope is always happy, even when it is entirely without justification.

I did my best to understand what Red Sox fans felt. I don't claim to have succeeded, because I think that outsiders can only expect to have a very partial understanding. As a sympathetic New Yorker who was not a Yankee fan, I imagined that Red Sox love embodied the bleak yet beautiful mystery of New England. It had something in it of the hope and fear of the early Puritan settlers. It seemed to me to be like the love a shy, lonely mill hand, in a red brick mill town would have for a beautiful, indifferent woman. Red Sox love was a suspicious love. It was deep, but it expected, and had already accepted, the inevitability of betrayal. It was a dream of happiness in the mind of someone who is convinced that happiness is just a dream. It was powerful and complicated and older than the Boston Red Sox.

Mets love, by contrast, felt like something a puppy would feel for its master. Mets fans were as loyal as dogs and their love was like that of a stubbornly optimistic child. But there was nothing dog-like or kid-like about Red Sox love. It was all grown-up and painfully human. It was tragic and it was scary. To be perfectly honest, as a Mets fan who had just begun to root for the Red Sox, I didn't like it. I wanted the freaky spell or curse to go away, to be wiped away by the kind of success that such a good team, and such a dedicated fan base deserved. I didn't think it would take long. I had never seen a Mets team with a lineup like what the Red Sox had in the late '70s. I wanted the Red Sox to win it all once so that these poor people could turn back into ordinary hopeful baseball fans.

After Sheila and I got married, our friends would ask us what would happen if the Mets and the Red Sox ever faced each other in the World Series. I remember calculating that, all things being equal, the odds against any two teams facing each other in the World Series was 143 to 1. There was less than a 50 percent chance that it would happen in our lifetime. When both of our teams made the playoffs in 1986, I still didn't think that it was going to happen. The odds were 3 to 1 that it wouldn't. As I watched the fifth game of the American League playoffs, and the Red Sox were behind 5–2 with two outs in the ninth inning, I thought about how interesting a New York–California World Series would be. Then the Red Sox, on homers by Don Baylor and Dave Henderson, scored four runs to take the lead. Though the Angels tied it in the bottom of the ninth, the Red Sox won it in the 11th and of course they would go on to win the next two games and the pennant.

After the Red Sox came back from the dead in the fifth game of the Championship Series, I wondered what Charlie, my father-in-law, was feeling. I called him as soon as the game was over. He hadn't watched one of the greatest moments in Red Sox history. At the beginning of the ninth, he had gone out to his barn to work in his workshop, to spare himself the pain. I warn you. Mets fans will not be able to understand this. Red Sox fans will.

So the Mets–Red Sox series started. Everything was fine between us. We rooted for our teams and that was that. But the Series was nothing like what it should have been. You could hardly recognize the teams from the way they were playing. People wondered if the Red Sox and the Mets had been exhausted by their struggles against the Angels and the Astros. All I know is that late in the evening of October 25, we were sitting on our couch in our little living room in Hoboken, New Jersey, boyhood home of Sinatra, in an apartment on a street that looked more like old New York than most streets in New York. There had been a carnival atmosphere in Hoboken all day. You saw Mets flags and Mets banners everywhere. But now, as we watched the game on our little black-and-white set, behind the Venetian blinds that blocked our view of the street, we saw the Red Sox, in the top of the tenth inning, take a 5–3 lead. In the bottom of the tenth, we saw Wally Backman and Keith Hernandez quickly and weakly fly out.

It now looked as if the impossible thing was going to happen. The Red Sox were going to win the World Series. Sheila couldn't wait to call her parents, and both sets of grandparents. I was happy for her, genuinely happy for her, in spite of my disappointment. I felt that there was no question that the Mets were the better team. But hey, the 1973 Reds were a lot better than the 1973 Mets. The 1969 Orioles were one of the best teams of all time. Enough said. The Mets had blown this one. It was their fault. They had played a weird series. Yes, I was disappointed, but this was the way it was going to be. And the Mets were so good, and so young, they would have plenty of chances to win the World Series in the next few years. I could live with this. I would not cry. And it would be easy for me to be civil and enthusiastic on the phone to my in-laws.

Locked in their eternal embrace, every Mets and Red Sox fan knows what happens next. Gary Carter hits a single. Kevin Mitchell hits a single. Calvin Schiraldi, exhausted, remains on the mound. Ray Knight hits a single. Stanley replaces Schiraldi, and with the count two and two on Mookie Wilson, after two foul balls, Stanley throws an inside breaking pitch that gets past the catcher, Rich Gedman. Mitchell scores to tie the game. The runners move up. There are two more foul balls. Then Mookie hits a mysterious little bouncer down the first base line, throws his bat away, and starts running with all his might. Old and hurting, Bill Buckner watches the strange ball bounce towards him. He knows how fast Mookie can run. When the ball comes, he bends to receive it. It bounces, as all will know for all time, through his legs and down the right field line.

What I hear at this moment is the immense and glorious thunder of voices united in triumph. Hoboken erupts. People open their windows and scream into the night air. I hear voices on the street, the sounds of people running and laughing and cheering. My parents had always said that when Brooklyn won the pennant, there was dancing in the streets. I always liked the idea of dancing in the streets, of the city becoming a big family celebration, all because of baseball. People outside our Venetian blinds were, I guess, dancing in the streets. I was shaking with excitement, pressing my lips together to prevent any sound from escaping. Sheila had dropped to her knees in front of the television and it looked as if she was praying. But she wasn't, she was weeping, and mourning, and keening. I put my hands on the shoulders of the woman I loved more than the whole world combined. I was amazed that she let me touch her. There was nothing I could say to console her. I just moved with her rhythm of rocking back and forth. Of course I was not sad. But I felt in her shoulders and sobs the bottomless sadness of the Red Sox fan. I knew she was right when she said through her tears that neither of her grandfathers would live to see the Red Sox win the World Series. There was no point in saying that maybe they would. Sure it was possible that the Red Sox could win the Series next year, or the year after. The grandfathers might live for quite a few more years. They did, in fact. But of course they never saw the Red Sox win the World Series. I knew they wouldn't. I knew she was right. Just as she and I and everyone else knew that the Mets would win the 1986 World Series, even though there was still one more game to play. I don't think there is any such thing as fate. I think it is a ridiculous concept. The only thing that ever gives me a sense that there might be such a thing as fate is baseball.

Sheila didn't watch the seventh game. I watched it myself. I saw the Mets fall behind 3–0. And I remember the eerie, yet totally matter-of-fact sense I had that this was nothing to worry about. Never before and never since have I been as certain that the Mets were going to win a game in which they were three runs behind. At breakfast on the morning of the seventh game, Sheila announced that she would never again be a baseball fan. She said that she had wasted enough time and emotional energy on the sport, and that it wasn't worth it. I said of course it wasn't worth it, by itself. The time and the emotional energy we wasted on it were what made it worth it. She looked at me as if I was crazy. I don't remember exactly what she said, but I do remember that it was profane and dismissive.

Sheila never came back to the game. Charlie still follows them but he loves and hates them as much as he always has. Over time, his loving bitterness has grown barnacles. It is something old and hard and sharp and, I guess, New England-y. In 2004, the man who had missed the comeback against the Angels stopped watching the Championship Series after the Yankees won the first three games. When he heard that the Red Sox had won their first game, he said, "So what, they're still going to lose it, after the season they had." He said the same thing when they won the second game, and he said the same thing after the third. Only after the Red Sox won the fourth game and the pennant was he glad. And he was pleased to see the Red Sox beat the Cardinals in four games in the World Series. But he would not lose himself in contemplation of the unimaginable glory of the most dramatic eight game winning streak in postseason history. He wondered why, if they could do it now, they couldn't have done it before.

Baseball is not necessarily about having fun and being happy. Neither is life. That makes no sense, of course, since it seems as if a game should be different from life. It should give us a rest from it. But that's not what baseball gives us. Baseball fans aren't looking for a way to escape their lives. They're looking, I think, for something that can run parallel to life, and look like it, something that has ups and downs, pleasures and pains, but is clearer and easier to grasp than life is. I see so much of myself in my baseball. Charlie must see himself in his. Sheila got tired of looking in this mirror and thinking that what it showed her was real.

Mookie Wilson

Mookie Wilson is on almost everyone's list of favorite Mets of all time. He was, of course, the player who gave us the single most exciting moment in Mets history. Yet Mookie is not popular because of that moment, in the way that Al Weis is popular because of what he did in the 1969 World Series. Mookie is popular because he had a career that is exemplified by what happened in the bottom of the tenth inning of the sixth game of the 1986 World Series. He hit a ball that should have been fielded. But what he hit was not what was happening. What was happening was Mookie running down the line, with an explosive and irresistible conviction that he would make it to first base. Because he believed he would make it to first, the fans believed he would make it, and it certainly looks on the replay as if he convinced Bill Buckner as well. And so it happened. Throughout his career, Mookie was always more than what he did. But he wasn't creating an illusion. By seeming to be more than what he was, he was more than what he was.

The Mets at the beginning of the eighties were a dismal team. Then Mookie arrived. He was eager, hopeful, sweet, and fast. He had the same real name as the great Royals centerfielder, Willie Wilson, and his speed and his flashes of brilliance encouraged us to believe that someday he would play like Willie Wilson. Mookie would hit over .300, he'd hit over 20 home runs, and he'd steal more than 50 bases. Well, he never hit over

.300. He never hit more than 10 home runs in a season. He did steal more than 50 bases a couple of times. But if Mookie had any kind of real greatness, it didn't show up on paper. In fact, anyone thumbing through the *Baseball Encyclopedia*, looking at the Mets in the eighties, will not be able to understand why Mookie is still spoken of with love and awe, while Kevin McReynolds is forgotten.

What was it that made Mookie so wonderful? I have an impression that he was a good clutch hitter but I don't really know if the statistics would bear that out. I have a sense that he made some great and important catches, but I also remember that he wasn't considered a particularly good outfielder. Mookie was often called a "sparkplug" as a lead-off hitter, but he didn't walk very often, and he struck out a lot, so he really couldn't have been such a terrific leadoff hitter. There's no controversy about the fact that Mookie was a great guy and that he had a wonderful attitude, but we all know that those attributes will only get you so far. Sure, Mookie was a good ballplayer and he never had the kind of genuinely bad season that would cause you to lose faith in him. The speed really was something else and we all remember him running down balls in the outfield, making it from first to third on a ground out, stealing home a couple of times, and hitting a couple of inside the park home runs. But Mookie wasn't as good as you would think he was, considering how large he looms in the memories of Mets fans. Why was Mookie forgiven the fact that his career was, well, a little disappointing? Why did we love him so much, when we have not warmed to several players who were better than he was?

I think that at some level all Mets fans know the answer to this question. Mookie seemed to enjoy playing the game of baseball more than anyone ever has. He enjoyed it as a fan would, who had sold his soul to the devil and was put into the body of a ballplayer. You weren't in awe of him. You identified with him. He represented your own enthusiasm for the game. He had all of your nervous, hopping ecstasy, your imaginary happiness to be on the field, your perpetual expectation of amazing miracles. It was as if he was what his childish nickname implied. It was as if he was the childish soul of every fan.

By playing well enough, and by being so happy to play, Mookie got us to believe in him. And because we believed in him, we began to think that the Mets could win. And sure enough, soon after Mookie came up, the Mets began to win, big time, and it seemed at some level to be because of him, because of his energy, his smile, his sense of being perfectly in tune with the fans and their love. Actually, the Mets were winning because of the far more talented, yet personally flawed players around him. But Mookie was our emotional link with that mid–eighties team. He was the link between the drought and the flood. He was the most loved Met in their greatest era and he was the only Met of that era to have fully paid his cellar-dwelling dues. And so when he turned a little grounder into an unfathomable miracle that gave the great team the World Championship they deserved but were so screwed up in the head they almost didn't get, it seemed perfect and right. And it was.

We savor our memories of Mookie. We remember how we always went "Mooooooo!" every time he came to the plate, and how that was so funny because there was no way in hell we would ever boo him. Mookie was not one of the greatest Mets, but he was the guy with the flag. And for the fans, the guy with the flag is important. He focuses our fandom. We jump up and down with him. At the end of a great game, we hug the other players with his arms. He proves that however much baseball may really be a battle of measurable forces, to the fan it will never really seem that way.

Keith Hernandez

Keith Hernandez played a slow and awkward man's position with a quick and steady grace. He took mental control of the ball as soon as it left the hitter's bat. If the ball was hit to the right side of the infield, it wouldn't pass. Keith's shoulders told you that he had it covered. And if anything was complicated, if it was ever unclear who should take a pop up or who should field a grounder and who should cover a base, Keith would know exactly what to do. He'd know immediately. There was none of the lumbering indecision you often saw at first base. Keith seemed to be too smart to make a bad or an awkward play.

Watching Keith Hernandez play first base is one of the all-time great pleasures of being a Mets fan. It was particularly fun because it was something unique. You knew what it was like to watch a great shortstop or centerfielder. You had seen enough of them and you could compare them. Watching a great defensive first baseman was a genuine novelty. You'd never seen it done before. So that's how that position can be played! You can move like that? You have enough time to do that? Who would have thought it?

Keith played first base because he had the instincts and reflexes of a great defensive shortstop, but he didn't have the speed or flexibility. He was as good as he was because he knew how to use his talents and adjust to his limitations. You saw the same thing in the way that Keith hit. He was a great hitter, but he wasn't a slugger, like the slow, powerful giants they normally stick at first base. He couldn't try for the big arch. So he found a way of hitting that made the outfield seem enormous. His swing was as straight and as smooth as an arrow's flight. His line drives were taut and focused. They were impatient and they would find the ground, or a corridor to the wall, before anybody could get near them. And so a man who never hit 20 home runs would always have about 100 RBIs. He'd hit his .310, and his 35 doubles. He was terrific.

As you watched Keith play, you couldn't read him. You couldn't read Strawberry either, but that was because Darryl was a mystery to everyone, including himself. Keith was different. You couldn't read him because he had a zone of privacy. He was a smart man who understood that he had to work very hard, at a troubled moment in his life, to compartmentalize things so that he could do what he had to do. There was his divorce. There was having to testify about his own past drug use. Keith's brilliant and consistent play throughout the 1984–6 seasons reminds you that people sometimes have the resources they need to avoid being distracted by personal problems. This is what was most unique about Keith: his magnificent talent for concentration. This is the sort of person who can steady himself by doing crossword puzzles. This is the kind of player who can give you the same exact level of performance year after year. This is the kind of player who will be deadliest in the clutch.

But Keith's hard-earned control never turned him into a pressure cooker. He knew how to let loose. He knew when. He knew not to pretend. He had the soul of a writer more than that of an ordinary baseball player. He knew when discipline was and wasn't the same thing as control. He knew that demons had to be put in their place, but he knew that you couldn't kill them, because that wasn't possible and besides, you needed them.

Somebody as focused, mature, talented, and real as Hernandez is inevitably going to become a leader and a model in any group. You saw that the 1986 Mets were Hernandez's team, with Davey Johnson's wise but wary permission. Everyone on the team always said that Keith was the best leader, the best team captain. Fans could watch him take charge: barking at the other infielders, going to the mound to get things back on track. Sometimes he looked like a commanding officer. Sometimes he looked like an orchestra conductor. The job got done. The team was led, by smooth, quiet Johnson in the dugout, and by Keith, tightly-wound, in command on the field. But if Keith could lead beautifully on the field and in the dugout, it was a harder thing for him to lead off the field and away from the dugout. It is hard for someone like Keith to serve as a personal model to people who don't have his discipline and maturity. Keith was fallen, but he was not falling. And the wisdom you have after the Fall is notoriously hard to communicate.

In the end, Keith was the man because Keith was so cool. And his cool gave the whole weird team an erotic aura. Almost every heterosexual female Mets fan I knew was in love with Keith. And in 1986, I often passed a gay bar on Christopher Street that had a great picture of Keith, from behind, blown up in the window. You didn't have to find men sexy to see that Keith was sexy. He was very handsome according to the hairy mustached standards of the '80s. But the main thing that made him so appealing was the fact that he was a grown-up and not an inflated little boy, as so many talented ballplayers are. Keith had edges and irony. He had a lot going on but he was finding his way. He came across as a genuinely interesting human being who wanted to give us the full benefit of his unique talent. You saw that for Keith playing baseball was a lot of work. But you also saw that it was keeping him sane.

Darryl Strawberry

I saw Darryl Strawberry's first major-league at bat, in May 1983, at Shea. As soon as I saw his body in motion, I knew, like everyone else, that he was destined for greatness. Until I saw Strawberry, I had never seen anything made entirely of angles flow. He hit a very long foul ball that made everyone stand and scream. He struck out. He struck out a lot at the beginning. But you knew he would be all right. He looked like a dinosaur just hatched from an egg. It was going to take him some time to get all of his parts moving together in the way they were supposed to.

When Strawberry came up, he had a look in his eyes, a look that I see in photos of me when I was two and my sister was born and I must have been unsure if my parents would continue to love me. You knew Strawberry would not be great until that look went away. It never did. He holds most of the Mets' offensive records and there were several sustained stretches in which he was fully as good a hitter as Babe Ruth or Ted Williams. He was an integral part of the best Mets team ever. But we all know that he didn't really do it. He never got over the bar of our perfectly legitimate expectations. He never became as good as he looked or as good as he gave us hope he could be.

Maybe if we had never had those expectations, we would have been happy with him. What was there not to be happy with? For eight seasons, he was our dominant offensive player and one of the best in the game. No one that I recall has ever excited an entire stadium more than Darryl did when he would come to the plate. You always expected something spectacular. And so often you would see the smooth and perfect swing send the ball into a dimension that no other hitter knew about. He was famous for hitting physical objects in other stadiums, clocks and ceilings and such, that no one had ever hit before. He'd hit his home run and you would watch him standing there, puzzled and wondering. You'd see his tall, remarkable body, alone and exposed, with his head shaped like a bullet, as he watched without emotion the ball leave the park. Strawberry's home runs were sublime, but there was always something eerie about them.

Darryl was haunted by his enormous talent which he did not understand and could not control. He was haunted by the expectations we had of him. We could see what he could do but it looked as though he couldn't. It looked as though he was struggling to survive in a reality that felt magical to us but not to him. As if to represent this, he was haunted by numbers. It was uncanny how in every one of his seasons, his numbers were good but always fell just short of where you thought, all season, they'd end up. In five of his seasons with the Mets it seemed as if he was going to hit thirty home runs, but he ended up with 29, 29, 27, 26, and 26. In his three best seasons, it seemed all year as if he was going to hit forty, but he ended up with 39, 39, and 37. Five times he came within just a couple of homers or stolen bases of having a 30–30 season, but he actually did it only once. In 1987, Darryl almost became the first player in major league history to have more than 40 home runs and 40 stolen bases. But he ended up with 39 home runs and 37 steals. He did drive in over a hundred runs three times, but three times he came just barely short. As this kind of thing happened over and over, you couldn't help but wonder if there were brakes inside Darryl that pulled him back just as he got close to certifiable greatness. And then you'd feel like a jerk for being somehow dissatisfied with 39 home runs or 97 runs batted in. Still, Met fans, who would cheer enthusiastic players who didn't have half of these totals, couldn't escape the impression that Darryl was withholding something. He was not being Willie Mays on purpose.

The reason we felt this is because it was in large part true. There was something wrong with Darryl. I don't know what and I can't speculate. There was something wrong that led him to drink and to drugs, to smack his wife and to smack Keith Hernandez after a photo shoot. There was a nauseating revolving spectacle of screw ups and apologies. The home runs continued. But you lost faith that you would ever see all you dreamed of seeing when someone unfortunately called a troubled and depressed eighteen-year-old kid a black Ted Williams. But I don't want to dwell on this. I just want to remember the grand parabolas, higher than anyone else's. I want to remember the palpable terror of the other teams, the homers that would come in clusters, or at just the right moment, like the one in the eighth inning of the seventh game of the '86 series, which finally declared that the historic match of the Mets and the Red Sox was over. I want to remember, with admiration and pity, what this fragile wreck of a man brought us in his eight seasons. He was touched by something. He brought us to the edge. We were thrilled. But he couldn't take it.

1987

The 1986 Mets were not fated to become a dynasty. But they had too much talent to be a flash in the pan. In 1987, the 1986 Mets were still intact in most ways, and in several ways, they were improved. In 1987, Strawberry had his best year and Howard Johnson played like a superstar. Kevin Mitchell was traded for Kevin McReynolds. Trying to get rid of trouble, the Mets gained one hell of a left fielder.

McReynolds was a problem case, for Mets fans. He was terrific. He had real style with a glove and he was a superb and remarkably consistent hitter. He wasn't an asshole, like, say, Kingman. Or a weird scary stranger, like George Foster. It's just that with McReynolds you kept knocking and he wouldn't answer. You kept calling out to him and he wouldn't turn around. You waved at him and he wouldn't see you. He wanted to be admired for his work on the field but he didn't think anything else was part of the bargain. Well, we admired him all right. Was that all there was going to be? Was he only going to work and pay the bills? Didn't he realize we had other needs? Other players did. However good McReynolds was, this wasn't good. This was an unconsummated relationship.

Every time McReynolds was interviewed he talked about how

uncomfortable he was with big cities and city ways and big city people. He talked about how he just wanted to be back home with simple country folks, doing a lot of duck hunting. Hey, we could have been real downhomey folks if he only gave us a chance. We didn't mind that he was from Arkansas. Some of our best friends are from Arkansas. Lots of small town Southern boys make it big in New York. Why was he so afraid of us?

Eventually, Kevin's alienation was so intense that to show him that New York was good for something, the Mets' publicity people took him on a tour of the studios of his favorite soap opera. His favorite soap opera! Once we accepted the indignity of having to prove to someone that New York's existence was justified because it was the place soap operas came from, we couldn't help but marvel at this man. How much goddamn duck hunting do they do in soap operas? How down-homey are those people? I haven't watched a lot of soap operas but something tells me that the answers to these questions are "none" and "not very." Somebody should have just told McReynolds that the people in the stands at Shea were like the people in the soap operas. We're a lot more like people in soap operas than the people in Arkansas are. Maybe that would have given him a way of imagining us. But he never did imagine us. And I guess we gave up trying to imagine him.

So Kevin came in '87, and he was a quiet reliable almost–MVP blank at the center of the team. But you can't blame him for the fact that the Mets won sixteen fewer games in 1987 than they won in 1986. You can't blame Strawberry or Hojo, or Keith, who was Keith as always. You can't blame Gary Carter, who had begun to decline but still contributed offensively and called a great game. McReynolds, Johnson, and Strawberry more than made up for Carter's drop-off. And I don't buy the idea that the Mets weren't as good in 1987 because they didn't hell around as much. Cashen was right not to give a two-year contract to Knight. And with McReynolds, we didn't miss Mitchell.

The Mets weren't as good in 1987 because the pitching staff slumped. Ojeda, who had a career year in 1986, was out for most of the season and no one effectively replaced him. Gooden didn't pitch until June because he was in drug rehab. Darling and Fernandez dropped down a peg, maybe because there was more pressure on them with Ojeda and Gooden gone. The great matched pair in the bullpen were nowhere near as good in '87 as they had been in '86. Still, the Mets won 92 games. If any one of the things that went wrong with the pitching staff hadn't gone wrong, the Mets would have made up the three games that, in the end, separated them from the Cardinals.

Nineteen eighty-seven should be remembered as the year the Mets made a terrific comeback in spite of their pitching woes. After limping along, six or seven games behind the Cardinals for most of the season, they turned it on, powered by Strawberry's gargantuan final month, and they came as close as a game and a half. They were one out away from a victory in the first game of a crucial September series against the Cardinals, a victory that would have put them just a half game behind, when Terry Pendleton hit one of the two home runs that every Mets fan in the eighties still feels as a once searing, now dull pain in his or her gut. The Mets would keep fighting. But it would not happen. It was a great run. But people don't talk or think about it much because the peak of the volcano never broke the surface of the water. It came just short.

So what people remember about 1987 is that Darryl was a pain in the ass, Gooden was in rehab, Kevin McReynolds replaced some of the energy of the team with a numb quiet, and 1986 did not repeat itself. It isn't fair but that's the way it is.

1988

The year 1988 wasn't disappointing. I wring my hands when people don't give this season its due because it was one of the best Mets seasons ever. In 1988, the Mets won as many games as they won in 1969. The only year in which they won more was 1986.

In 1988, the Mets scored more runs and gave up fewer runs than any other team in the National League. It is actually rare for a team to do both of these things in a single year. When a team does this, they dominate. The 1988 Mets dominated. Their offense was terrific, almost as good as the amazing offense in 1987. Strawberry was so exciting and McReynolds was making you happy even if he wouldn't make eye contact. But the real story of 1988 was the return of the pitching staff to its 1986 level. Gooden, Darling, Fernandez, and Ojeda all had fine seasons. Randy Myers emerged as a better relief pitcher than either McDowell or Orosco, who was traded away to the Dodgers. And David Cone had one of the best seasons in baseball history, a season that was comparable to the best seasons of Dwight Gooden and Tom Seaver.

The 1988 season was great and happy. Hernandez and Carter were now in decline, but they could still lead the troops and remind everyone of the recent and glorious heritage. You began to feel that they were not indispensable, not with young pitching this good, not with bright future stars like Gregg Jefferies, who came up in September and played so well that baseball card collectors were hoarding his rookie cards. There was a little bit of excitement in the middle of the 1988 season as the Pittsburgh Pirates played well and got within hailing distance. But the Pirates faded and the Mets had a bountiful September, coasting to a beautiful finish, with 100 wins, 15 games ahead of Pittsburgh.

Everyone expected that the Mets would get what they deserved: their second World Championship in three years. They were much better than the Dodgers, who couldn't hit. The Dodgers' pitching was good and Orel Hershiser was having a great season and was in the middle of a historic scoreless inning streak. But even the Dodgers' pitching was not as good as the Mets'. The team as a whole was just not that impressive. The Dodgers had lost ten of the eleven games they played against the Mets during the regular season.

As everyone knows, the Mets lost to the Dodgers in the 1988 playoffs. I'm sorry that happened. I'm really sorry that happened. I remember what it felt like when Mike Scioscia hit that ninth-inning home run to tie the fourth game. The Mets had been up two games to one and they were within seconds of being up three games to one. When Scioscia's homer barely cleared the center field wall, I felt that change in the universal wind, that feeling that Red Sox fans must have had as the ball went through Buckner's legs.

It's weird how hope drains when something like this happens. Surely it was not inevitable that Kirk Gibson would hit the home run that would win that game for the Dodgers in the twelfth. Surely it was not inevitable that the mediocre Dodgers would then go on to win two out of three from the perfect Mets. Even after Scioscia's home run, I didn't completely lose hope. I never completely lost hope. But I had that horrible nausea familiar to baseball fans. The nausea of the Orioles in '69. The nausea of the Reds in '73. I had felt the rip. I had heard the harsh, tearing sound. It is hell. When what you try to wish away finally happens, all you can do is stand over the sweet, dead thing and cry.

The End of the Eighties

The greatest Mets team of all time, the Mets of the eighties, the Davey Johnson Mets, would never get there again. Nineteen eighty-eight was it. The team stayed pretty good for another two years and it might have won something if it weren't for some of the crap that was happening. Sid Fernandez, Howard Johnson, Kevin McReynolds, David Cone, Randy Myers, Frank Viola, John Franco, and Darryl Strawberry all had terrific years. Greg Jefferies was exciting, even though you knew everyone on the team hated him. But Hernandez and Carter had reached the end. Mookie and Lenny and Roger McDowell were traded away. You could tell that the atmosphere on the team was terrible. The Jefferies thing was a distraction. Juan Samuel was a bust. A full-time psychiatrist couldn't solve any of our head cases. As a fan, you felt completely helpless. These were our guys. You knew what they could do. Sure they had a right to have problems, but anybody can have problems. Not everybody can be part of a championship baseball team. How could these guys let something as banal as their personal problems and private animosities get in the way of doing what they needed to do to make millions of people happy?

It really was all over when Scioscia hit his dark and horrible home run.

Should we be disappointed? This is a question a lot of people ask. And there is a consensus, it seems, twenty years later, that as great as they were, the Mets of the Eighties were underachievers.

This is bullshit. Has anyone ever bothered looking at what other teams do and have done? I mean other teams beside the Yankees. Once again we are haunted by the bigger brother. Only the Yankees ever do anything like win a couple of World Championships in a row and they only do that every few decades. But then everybody remembers it and talks about Yankee dynasties and the dynasties all get connected as if they were a continuous stream of triumph. But this isn't what it's like for most baseball teams and it isn't even what it is really like for the Yankees.

Most team baseball triumphs are not World Championships. Especially not now, when a team that beats out every other team in its division has only one chance in eight of winning the World Series. In the eighties, the chance was one in four, but there was no Wild Card and only four teams out of twenty-four, instead of eight teams out of thirty made the playoffs. Had there been a Wild Card title in the eighties, the Mets would have won it four times: in 1984, 1985, 1987, and 1990.

This fabulous, unusual, and profoundly dramatic team had seven terrific years in a row. That doesn't happen often to any franchise. That is a good run. There are some trophies. One World Championship, one pennant, and two division titles. Fewer than ten games over seven seasons going the other way would have given us two or more World Championships and four or five division titles. But this "almost" business is true for every good or great team. Baseball is about hope, and hope is meaningless unless the natural condition of life is disappointment.

I am disappointed that the Mets of the '80s didn't win more. But I remember what I saw and what I felt during those seven years. It was a beautiful time. Even with, and partly because of the disappointments, it is a great story, sad and wonderful. It is part of my life and I am so happy to have shared it with millions of other people.

The Mets in the Early Nineties

The early 1990s were the worst period in Mets history. The Mets had been this bad before but they had been bad for reasons you understood, and however bad they had been, you liked the guys on the team. The Mets in the sixties were bad because they were an expansion club and the rules for expansion clubs didn't allow the Mets to get enough good players right away. But I loved the guys who played for the Mets in the sixties. They didn't win, but they were fun. The Mets of the late seventies and early eighties weren't fun, and I hated M. Donald Grant and I laughed at Lorinda and Bebe and Whatever De Roulet. But I really liked Steve Henderson and Craig Swan and Joel Youngblood and Doug Flynn and Lenny Randle and even loopy Willy Montanez. There were bozos on that team, like Hebner, but there were a lot of guys I liked and as we got closer to being good again, there were even guys like Mookie Wilson and Hubie Brooks whom I loved.

The Mets in the early nineties were an incomprehensible disaster. The team was willing to spend money. They were willing to make big trades. At the end of the eighties, they still had a nucleus of talent to build upon. Like most fans, I don't understand enough about front office decision-making to know who was responsible, but it seemed to me as if everything they proceeded to do was stupid, as if they were buying and trading baseball cards and not human beings. How could you root for people like Vince Coleman, Eddie Murray, and Bobby Bonilla? How could they think we would root for such people? When the trading and buying smoke cleared, we were left with a team of Kingmans. Nobody gave a shit. Most of what we had left from the eighties had been given away or allowed to leave. Sure he was a pain, but what was so wrong with Darryl that we wouldn't sign him for what we would eventually pay Murray? Gooden was still here. But what was he now? He had gone from being a mysterious disappointment to being a mysterious disappointment with a torn rotator cuff. Cone and Fernandez stuck around for awhile, but they were gone soon. Saberhagen and Franco were good, but what was the point?

The Mets in the early nineties were like a balloon losing air. There is no sense that anyone has of the early nineties "team." There were no veteran leaders like Hernandez, Carter, or Clendenon. And the managers didn't give the team any identity, as Hodges or Johnson had given a character and a shape to their teams. We all loved Buddy Harrelson as the great shortstop of our first glory years. But he clearly didn't have any managerial talent. Jeff Torborg seemed out of his league and he had nothing to work with. Dallas Green was an asshole.

Worst of all, there was nothing to hope for. How good could this team get? These were sour, unhappy years and following the seven great years from 1984 to 1990, they were very hard to take. I continued to watch and listen. I didn't go to very many games. Rooting for the Mets in this period was like being stuck to flypaper in the old cartoons. You couldn't get it off. But it did nothing for you.

Finally, in '94 and '95, there were some faint stirrings of promise. Rico Brogna, Jason Isringhausen, Bill Pulsipher, and Paul Wilson all looked like the real thing, like the nucleus of the future. But then they got hurt or fizzled. You began to wonder if the Mets would ever be good again, in this century.

The Mets and Seinfeld

During the third season of Seinfeld, in 1992, Keith Hernandez appeared as himself in a two-part episode entitled "The Boyfriend." In an interview on the DVD release, Jerry Seinfeld says that this is his favorite episode. It is certainly one of the most famous of all Seinfeld episodes, which means that it has been seen over and over by everyone in the entire world. Whenever anyone asks Keith Hernandez whether he thinks he is more famous for having played baseball or for having been a character on Seinfeld, he says he thinks he is more famous for having been a character on Seinfeld.

There must be a lot of people who know very little about baseball who, when they think of the New York Mets, think of this episode. I like this, because I want the Mets to represent to the world the things I like most about New York. And *Seinfeld* has given the world a sympathetic and not entirely inaccurate view of New York. I think it is closer to the soul of New York than any other television show has ever been, with the possible exception of *Car 54*. Jerry Seinfeld is a New Yorker and an enormous New York Mets fan. His comedy reflects this. There seems to me to be something deeply Mets-like about *Seinfeld*.

Like rooting for the Mets, *Seinfeld* is all about living with failure and false starts. It is about maintaining your expectations regardless of how reliably life does not reward you. It is about the same things happening to you over and over again, without you ever realizing that you are stuck. It is about sabotaging yourself. But it is also about the way in which life is made bearable, even pleasant, by the affection you have for the things you know best, for the things you have always known, which you love mainly because you know them. Things like Pez dispensers and Superman Comics and Mr. Met and the Home Run Apple. This aspect of Jerry Seinfeld, the sweet, loyal, love of the familiar, is central to the spirit of Mets fans. We do not desert the crumbling stadium and all the silly things in it just as we do not desert the disappointing team. We can't imagine our lives without them.

The faces and gestures of the Mets fan are the faces and gestures of Seinfeld's stand-up comedy. We shrug as he does. And you know that facial expression where he scrunches the lower part of his face and seems to be saying that something is ridiculous but what is he supposed to do about it? That is our face. In the show, and in his routines, Seinfeld is a connoisseur of the ways in which reality and social custom stubbornly refuse to make sense. This is not a philosophical perspective you could associate with the New York Yankees.

But it is exactly right for Mets fans. Being a Mets fan is fun, even though it is often ridiculous and humiliating and it doesn't make sense. You ever notice how when the Mets get good, they always seem to screw something up? Why is that? Hey, how about Mr. Met? What is it with that stupid smile? Why is everybody so excited when they shoot the Pepsi t-shirts into the crowd? Do they even know what is on the t-shirt? The apple in the hat? Why does the apple come out of a hat? When are apples ever in hats? Rabbits are in hats, sometimes. But apples? What is that supposed to mean?

Yankee fandom, with all of its rewards, has an element of rationality about it. The Yankee universe makes sense. Winning is a good thing and losing is a bad thing. The Yankees win. Therefore it makes sense to be a Yankee fan.

With the Mets, it's more complicated. Just as it is on *Seinfeld*. Winning and losing are often intimately connected. You expect to lose, even as you are winning. You think you might win, even as you are losing. Winning has a way of turning into losing. Losing leads to winning, without any warning. And while winning is good, losing can be good too.

In "The Boyfriend" episode Jerry starts off by winning big. He meets Keith Hernandez, his favorite ballplayer, in a locker room. Hernandez recognizes him and tells him that he loves his comedy. What better thing could happen to Jerry? He is in love with Hernandez. And this episode is built around the dream of all baseball fans that the love we have for a ballplayer could be requited.

Elaine actually gets to go out with Keith because of the accidental fact that she is a woman. But she is more amused than impressed by the great ballplayer. Elaine is not a fan. She doesn't know who Mookie is and she is hearing about "Game 6" for the first time. Jerry feels the injustice and the waste of this. So many men and women are in love with Keith. And here he is going out with someone who doesn't care who he is. It is Jerry who should be able to go out with Keith. Keith should be his "boyfriend," not Elaine's.

Elaine likes to see what Jerry goes through when Keith doesn't call him for three days. She enjoys seeing how jealous Jerry gets when Keith cancels a date with him to go out with her. The way men treat women has always been a mystery to Elaine. But now she sees that men like Jerry care about their favorite sports figures in the way women care about the men with whom they have fallen in love. In his "relationship" with Keith, Jerry's emotions are engaged, his vulnerabilities are exposed, as they never are when he's just going out with a woman.

As fans, don't we dream of the players making us happy? Aren't we crushed when they don't? Aren't we a little shy around them at first? When we finally embrace them, don't we think about them all the time? Don't we need them? Aren't we wounded when we have a sense that they don't care about us? Don't we want them to know how much we care about them? Aren't we sure that they would like us, if only they knew us, and understood our affection? Regardless of our gender or our sexual orientation, we baseball fans are all involved with these guys in something that feels like a relationship. Of course it is a waste that a non-fan like Elaine gets to go out with Keith just because she is a woman.

Hernandez is perfect in his role. He has the illusion that he is a real person, just another guy living through a protracted late adolescence on the Upper West Side. He thinks he is a Seinfeld character! Keith is making a new friend and trying to go out with a woman. His fame is only something he will use to try to get into bed with Elaine. Confident that he can impress Elaine with his eleven Golden Gloves, he is as clueless and self-absorbed as all of the other men Elaine goes out with. The fact that he smokes gives her the out she always looks for.

Jerry's biggest hero becomes his friend. They plan to go to movies together. The fan's fantasy is achieved. But then Keith asks Jerry to help him move. Senselessly self-sabotaging as always, the man who is puzzled by the logic of all rules and customs once again insists on their inviolability. A man has to know another man for longer than this in order to have the right to make this request. Jerry refuses to help Keith move, only to have Newman and Kramer take his place after Jerry demonstrates, in a parody of Oliver Stone's film about the Kennedy assassination, that Keith could not have been the one who "ruined" Kramer's life by spitting on them after Newman insulted Hernandez after a game in 1987.

Something has happened, but you don't know what it is. You thought things were fine, but something you couldn't have seen coming turned it all around in a moment. The world has many moving parts, subplots that come together and then diverge. Miracles happen. George can go out with Marisa Tomei. But everything will collapse in an instant. You're helpless as you watch. You can't believe what you're seeing. But you always come back to the same living room, the same friends, the same coffee shop, because this is where you have always been and it is where you will always be.

The history of the Mets shapes the spirit of the Mets fan. We believe that anything is possible, but we know that anything can happen. We are lyrical and sentimental about what we've had because what we've had is all we've got. We are even lyrical about losing because if we weren't, we'd have to hang it up. We are happy right where we are, even if we know that there are other people having a lot more success and maybe more fun somewhere else. Jerry Seinfeld has given the world a pattern of our perspective.

He made a lot of money doing this in L.A. But as a lover of his own oldest, deepest, most familiar things, he had to come back here. Now he can do whatever he wants and what he wants to do is go to Shea. The TV cameras always find him, sometimes with a friend who is sometimes a celebrity. It's great to have him back. But he never left.

1997–1998

The Mets have a way of going from very bad to very good overnight. It's as if they don't believe in incremental development. This tendency for the team to come back very suddenly has conditioned Mets fans to think that miracles can happen even when it doesn't seem as if things could possibly be any worse.

The Mets went straight from very bad to very good in 1969 and in 1984. They did it again in 1997. The Mets won 88 games in 1997, after winning 71 in 1996. In retrospect, it is easy to see why the 1969 team was better than the 1968 team and why the 1984 team was better than the 1983 team. But when you think back on the 1997 team and compare it to the 1996 team, it is hard to understand what happened. What happened, perhaps, was the new manager, the weird and very articulate Bobby Valentine. I loved having Bobby Valentine as the manager of the Mets. I enjoyed the way he approached managing as if it were a combination of rocket science and performance art. He was unpredictable, self-dramatizing, and imaginative. He did so many smart things but then inevitably, when it was least expected, he would do or say something stupid. The Mets teams of the late '90s, with their brilliance and their tendency to self-sabotage, may have been reflecting Valentine's personality. Or maybe this correspondence was just a coincidence. Who knows? Valentine, in any case, knocked things off balance. Somehow he turned a not-so-good team into a genuinely impressive one that came within a few games of winning the Wild Card.

In one way, the revival of the Mets in the second half of the '90s didn't follow the pattern of any previous Mets revival. In the past, new players would develop or be acquired and there you'd go. In the late '90s, most of the fine players who brought the Mets back would be gone by the time the Mets came all the way back. Lance Johnson, Bernard Gilkey, Jeff Kent, Todd Hundley, Jose Vizcaino, Butch Huskey, Mark Clark, Brian McRae, and Carl Everett could have been the nucleus of a fine team. But they were just the opening act.

Nineteen ninety-seven was so exhilarating because the Mets hadn't been good for seven years, and they hadn't felt promising and exciting in about nine. But in the memory, 1997 now serves now as a prelude to 1998, and both seasons are remembered as a prelude to 1999 and 2000, in the way that 1984 and 1985 have been reduced to opening acts for 1986. It was in 1998 that the Mets brought in Olerud, Leiter, and Piazza, built a lead for the Wild Card, had an awful last week, and ended up winning 88 games for the second straight year. Once again, it looked as if the Mets were numerically haunted, just as they had been in the early '70s. This time, the number was 88 instead of 83. And 1998 was just like 1985, in that in the second season of a revival, the Mets fell just short of making it to the playoffs in one last losing week. If they had just won one of their last six games, just one, they would have won the Wild Card. If John Franco, our great reliever, our Mets fan since birth, had just played during the last week of the 1998 season the way he had played throughout the entire decade, we would have been in the playoffs for the first time in ten years. Do other teams come this close, and miss this often? Do other teams get knocked over by such ridiculous ironies? Do other teams compulsively repeat such freaky patterns?

As disappointing as it was, 1998 was a lot of fun. A fabulous team had been built around some mature and intelligent ballplayers. The coming of Mike Piazza had changed everything. It was like the coming of Seaver or the coming of Hernandez. Suddenly you knew there was a future. Piazza hit something like .350 for us in 1998. And so did the quiet, intense, slow, focused and wonderful John Olerud. You learned that year, from Olerud and Piazza, what hitting .350 actually meant, what it felt like in the middle of your batting order. It was a remarkable thing and it wasn't like anything I had ever seen before.

On the mound, we had a reliable, experienced ace, which we also hadn't had in a long time. The grunting, gritty Al Leiter, with his amazingly expressive face, was such a pleasure to watch, as was the sad and defensive but aggressively solid Rick Reed, who pitched his heart out as he tried to live down the fact that he had scabbed during the strike season of 1994. Our homegrown Edgardo Alfonzo, with his uncanny serenity, was beginning to show superstar promise. And Franco still grew his vegetables in the bullpen, emerging regularly to save the game.

The Mets were poised for another charge to the top, insofar as they ever charge to the top. The Mets do end up on top from time to time, but why is it that when they do, it never seems to have been properly anticipated? Who thought we would win in 1969 or 1973? Who expected us to dominate so completely in 1986 or 1988 or 2006? Why is it that when the Mets suddenly happen to have a really great season, all of their rivals collapse and scatter?

On the other hand, when the Mets charge the battlements, hoping to defeat a superior team on the top of the hill, something different happens. They blow the bugle, they have the ammunition, they have the men they need, and they scramble in the right general direction. But then there are land mines. The enemy is firing back. They aren't really scared but things start getting funny. They blow up some enemy tanks and take out some snipers but then freaky shit happens and it is chaos all over again. They are a formidable franchise, the Mets are, when they charge to the top.

The Atlanta Braves and the New York Yankees must have thought we were very funny.

1999

The Mets had a terrific team going into 1999. To Piazza and Leiter and the rest, the newly aggressive front-office had, in the off-season, added Robin Ventura, Ricky Henderson, and Orel Hershiser. The 1999 team had a style that was different from any previous Mets team. It was an older guy style, but it wasn't an over-the-hill, on-their-last-legs style. The players were mostly in a kind of late or lingering prime and they were interesting, stable, and three-dimensional people. They weren't consumed by the distractions of late adolescence. They had no destructive bad habits.

They were not the Eighties team. You had a vague sense that this was exactly the point. But these guys weren't boring. The front office must have understood that the Kevin McReynolds approach didn't work. Mets fans would accept players who knew who they were and who had regular bedtimes, but they couldn't enjoy guys who were boring. And so, the solid, sympathetic 1999 team was designed to prove to us that it is possible to be interesting without getting into trouble.

The 1999 team was also different from other Mets teams because it was built around offense. When good, the Mets had always been a pitching team in a pitcher's park, with a decent offense at best. In this lineup, it seemed as if everybody could hit for average. Much of the lineup could also hit for power and a couple of the guys were amazingly fast. The 1999 Mets scored 853 runs. The Mets had never been that good offensively. Also, when the Mets had been good in the past, the team had been built to some degree around youthful superstars. Not this year. Everything was different in 1999. The novelty was fun.

It took a while for the 1999 team to get its act together. They were 27–28 until general manager Steve Phillips, afraid to fire Valentine, fired Valentine's coaches. But from that point forward, everything was beautiful. Piazza was in his first full season as a Met, and there had never been a Met who could hit as well as he could. Piazza hit as Seaver had pitched, with a focused, secure sense that he had a brighter flame than anyone else and it was his responsibility to make it burn steadily. People talked that year about whether our infield was the best infield on any team ever.

Olerud, Alfonzo, and Ventura were all strong, reliable hitters, who, with Piazza, gave the Mets a middle of the order that was every bit as threatening as what we had in 1986. And the leaping, stretching, whipping brilliance of Ordonez at short was even better than anything Harrelson had given us in his prime. We had fast, unsettling players like the ancient Ricky Henderson and the vague young Roger Cedeno. We had appealing bench players with quirky reservoirs of talent, guys like Benny Agbayani, Todd Pratt, and Joe McEwing. And although the starting pitching was a little iffy, we had a relief staff good enough to pick up the slack. We still had Franco, and the younger, bigger and at that point terrifying Armando Benitez. We had Dennis Cook and we had the entertaining silliness of Turk Wendell, who would scowl and throw the rosin bag to the delight of all the kids in the crowd.

Nineteen ninety-nine, as I remember it, was one of the most fun Mets years ever. The team was good and it was filled with character and characters. And the year was really exciting. Because we didn't dominate. Or rather we dominated everybody, except the Atlanta Braves. That was the story of the season, in the end. We were better than everyone. But we weren't better than the Braves. And it was very important to the Braves to make sure that we understood this. Nineteen ninety-nine was the peak of our rivalry with Atlanta. It was amazingly exciting. The only rivalry with another team we have ever had that was anything like this was what we had with the Cardinals in 1985 and 1987. We had series with the Braves that felt like the World Series in August and September. There was all this hype, and psyching and taunting. There was us calling Chipper Jones "Laaarrrrrrrrryyyy!!!!!!" and him saying that after the Mets lost, we would all go put our Yankee hats on. It was high level horseshit, happy hollering hatred. And there was terrific baseball between two exceptionally classy teams. I'll never forget it.

Even though, for the most part, it was a rout. The Braves beat us in nine out of twelve regular season games and there was absolutely no way that we could beat them in their home stadium. There was no good reason for a team as good as the 1999 Mets to be so psyched out by a stupid stadium, but they were. And there was something else besides. The 1999 Mets had a compulsive rhythm. They would play beautifully and then they'd suddenly dig themselves a hole, fall into it, look like they were dead, and then miraculously spring back to life. This was infinitely annoying but it was also very exciting.

I remember one game at Shea where I saw the Mets fall six runs behind Greg Maddux. That means it's all over, right? But then they came roaring back and beat him. Even if the Mets normally lost to Atlanta, they would come back by beating other teams. By late September we were very close to the Braves, and we had a four game lead over Cincinnati for the Wild Card. Then we lost seven in a row. Huh? How does a team this good do that? We were headed for a disappointment even worse than 1988. We couldn't beat Atlanta now. And we were two games behind Cincinnati, with only three more to play.

Mike and the Mad Dog said that it was simply not possible for us to make up that two game deficit with each team playing only three more games. They told us to think of what had to be done. They urged us to do the math ourselves and they slapped their stinking pencils on the table. For this reason more than just about any other, I desperately wanted the Mets to do it. The Mets did their part, winning all three games against the Pirates. I was at the last game of the regular season at Shea, when Piazza was up with the bases loaded and the pitch flew past the catcher and Melvin Mora came racing home. Late that night I listened to the Milwaukee announcers, broadcasting from some strange, slow Midwestern world, announce a game in which Cincinnati, having lost two to the Brewers, came feebly back to tie us.

The next night was one of the pinnacles of Mets history. How often do you see a season come down to a single game? When Al Leiter took the mound, I saw in his face that he would pitch the game of his life that night. He did, although the problem with Al Leiter is that sometimes you would see that exact same look in his face and he wouldn't pitch the game of his life. It was an amazingly pitched game, a perfect two-hitter. Leiter was as dominant as Clemens when he was really on and I had a guilty and unpleasant moment of wondering whether Leiter might have been as good as Clemens if he was more like Clemens, if he wasn't so goddamn human and human-looking.

We won the Wild Card. Now we had to beat Arizona, which wasn't a better team than we were, but we all knew what "Arizona" meant, in that year of phantoms and psych-outs. It meant Randy Johnson, the best pitcher in the National League, a terrifyingly talented, thoughtful and decent man who happened to look like a preying mantis, or a gigantic psychopath in a low-budget horror film. The papers beat the hype drum. How could we get past Johnson? No one, I guess, had ever beaten a pitcher that good before. Could we expect this team to beat him, this team that could never find the moxie to win a baseball game in a certain stadium in Georgia? Analysts comforted us with the observation that we really only needed to win one of the two games played in Phoenix. That was a relief.

While we didn't exactly beat Johnson, we did beat the Diamond-backs in the first game of the series, which he started. Edgardo Alfonzo, after midnight in the East on a school night, hit a grand slam home run in the ninth inning off a relief pitcher to win the game. We lost the second game, but then we won the third. The fourth game, though, had all the makings of another Scioscia moment in Mets history. Our great young reliever, Armando Benitez, blew our 2–1 lead in the ninth by giving up a two-run double. We tied it in the bottom of the ninth. And then, in the bottom of the tenth, Todd Pratt won the series for us with a home run.

That was such a great moment. An Al Weis moment. A Benny Agbayani moment. A moment when a bench player reaches back and manages to scrawl his name in big letters on the wall of Mets history. Todd Pratt will always be remembered by Mets fans for that one swing of the bat, and for a famous hug a few days later.

And so now the season came back to the place it had never really left. To win the pennant, we had to beat Atlanta. Here was our chance for redemption. All we had to do was do what we hadn't been able to do all year long. But if we did it this time, the fact that we hadn't done it those other times wouldn't matter. And so we lost the first three games.

What do you do now? You say that the Mets are the team of miracles, and you ignore all the things they have done to put themselves in the position of needing so many miracles. Bobby Valentine, on the blackboard in the clubhouse, wrote "Why not?" He might as well have written "How?" or "Why?' but he refrained from doing so.

Sure enough, they pulled a game out, in incredibly dramatic fashion. Then they won another one, with Robin Ventura's grand-slam single in the bottom of the fifteenth inning, arguably the most exciting finish of any game the Mets have ever played except for the sixth game of the 1986 World Series. We were getting there. We could do it. We had the momentum on our side. Leiter took the mound in the sixth game and you saw on his face what you saw in the one-game playoff where he two-hit the Reds.

And he gives up five runs in the first inning. You knew the momentum had to have actually been on our side from the fact that we almost won this game. But even cosmic momentum has limited resources and perhaps, in some cases, limited patience.

The bullpen held and the Mets came back with three runs in the top of the sixth. But then Atlanta scored two more in the bottom of the sixth, to make it 7–3. The Mets managed four runs to tie the game in the top of the seventh, and then went ahead in the eighth, 8–7. But Franco, who had been great all year long, gave up the tying run in the bottom of the eighth. The Mets managed to take the lead again, 9–8, in the top of the tenth. Then it was Benitez's turn to let the game be tied, in the bottom of the tenth. The Mets didn't score in the top of the eleventh, and then in the bottom of the eleventh, poor Kenny Rogers gave up a leadoff double and a sacrifice bunt, walked two men intentionally to set up a double play or a force at any base, and then, on a 3–1 pitch, walked home Atlanta's pennant-winning run.

It had been an exciting season. It was fun. Losing, in the end, was not as painful as it might have been, since in spite of all their heroics, the Mets really had, without any possible controversy, lost the pennant. They won the Wild Card and they had beaten Arizona in the first series. They had won something, even if, years later, we still don't know exactly what to call it.

The Second Most Exciting Mets Game Ever

The second most exciting Mets game ever played was the fifth game of the 1999 National League Championship Series against the Atlanta Braves. After losing three close, heartbreaking games to Atlanta, the Mets had won the fourth game dramatically at Shea as John Olerud hit a two-run single in the ninth inning off of John Rocker.

Mets fans began to wonder if 1999 had one more comeback in it, or maybe two, since we might need another one in the World Series. Though we were still down three games to one, we began to believe that once again we had some sort of momentum. You knew that this was a crucial moment in Mets history and so, for the first time since the sixth game of the 1986 National League Playoffs, my parents and sisters and I decided that it was absolutely necessary that we watch a ballgame on television together.

And so we gathered in the den again. We joked about how it would be good luck for the Mets, since they had won that sixteen-inning game in the same room thirteen years before. We also couldn't help but notice that it was thirteen years later. In most ways, the den was exactly the same as it had been in 1986. The furniture, clocks, paintings, and shelves were all where they had been. But while the room in 1986 looked like the room of a late middle-aged couple, while it looked as if it had recently been the room of a whole family, the room in 1999 looked like something much more precarious. Everything really needed to be dusted and everything on the shelves had been pushed into weird angles by framed pictures of my daughter. The three-dimensional version of my daughter, age 8, was the only human addition to the scene. There were no subtractions, but my father sat very quietly in the armchair that had always been his. In 1986, he had been an active doctor in his early sixties taking a rare afternoon off. In 1999, you couldn't tell what he understood and what he didn't.

Alzheimer's destroys your ability to follow a baseball game. But it doesn't destroy your ability to look as if you're following a baseball game. All of your emotional gestures can still be performed, if you get the right cue. This is what made that afternoon so uncanny. My mother and my sisters and I were still there, deeply within the game. If we lost it, we were gone. If we won it, we would never forget it. And so we screamed with vindication and certainty as Olerud, now on fire as he emerged from a postseason slump, hit a two-run homer in the first. We were devastated when the Braves came back and tied the game. And we were up and down through all of the innings that followed, as the two teams played in a steady rain, with no one scoring. It was as if we were watching hand-to-hand combat in a jungle. Like most really exciting games, it is only pleasant to recall. The game itself, in real time, was hell.

In the thick emotion of that wet afternoon darkening into evening, my eight-year-old daughter and my seventy-five-year-old father were very much with us. They cheered when we cheered. They mimicked us, but they would not have known what to do without us. In our little den, we were all together. But it wasn't as it had been in 1986. It felt as if we were in some kind of vehicle lurching through time and space and we were holding on to each other as we all held on to the Mets.

We called out for a Chinese dinner, which took a bizarrely long time to arrive. We ate it on the little portable tables that hadn't been used for years. When we finished, it was the eleventh inning and I had to hit the road. It was Sunday. My daughter had school the next day. I couldn't stay any longer. I was sorry to have to leave, but I had to go, and I don't know how much more I could have taken in the den, waiting for the Mets to score a run, fearing that the Braves would score a run.

I left the den, but the game was still with me in the car. It continued, and no one scored. The game was stuck and it had begun to feel like the sixth game of the playoffs against the Astros in 1986. It assumed its own weird identity, its own uniqueness, as it crawled towards its historic indefinite length. I thought of how strange it would be that it would finally end when I was alone, in the rain and the darkness, with my daughter sleeping in the back seat.

As I drove on what seemed to be deserted highways, I thought of my father, and my daughter, and I tried to decide if baseball made life seem longer or shorter. In ways, I think, it makes life seem longer, because you have this sense of an infinite series of brightly lit evenings recalling other brightly lit evenings, summer afternoons that recall other summer afternoons. You have all these games you remember. And because the players' careers are like miniature human lifetimes, you remember more generations of players than you remember generations of people. So you feel as if you remember so much, as if you have seen so much of this long, continuing thing.

But then you think of how, over 40 years, you have only seen a few basic stories and only a few championships. At the rate at which championships come, you will only see a few more, unless you're a Yankee fan, and then they don't mean as much. You may never see another one. Driving home on that rainy evening, three months from the end of the century, I thought of how my daughter born in 1991 was going to see some decades of Mets baseball, in the second half of the twenty-first century, that I would not see. If she chose to pay attention.

If I could have seen those decades, I would have been able to understand them and follow them, just as I could have understood and followed baseball in the 1920s. There would be a lot about the late twenty-first century that I would not have been able to understand. But baseball would have been familiar. Baseball was always baseball, intact, complete, permanent, and youthful. While everything crumbled around it. Or at least changed.

When I got off at my final exit, it was the fifteenth inning and the Braves took the lead on a two-out triple. I did not think I could make it home by the end of the game. But as if he was doing it so that I could see the end of this ballgame, Shawon Dunston fouled off something like fifteen pitches. The endless nerve-wringing fouls felt like an image of the endless game itself and the apparently endless impossible season. The string of fouls ended with a single straight up the middle. Then Matt Franco walked as I got closer and closer to home, and Edgardo Alfonzo bunted the two runners over. As I pulled into the driveway, John Olerud took first base on an intentional walk and Todd Pratt came to the plate.

I turned off the engine and jumped out of the car and opened the back seat and lifted my sleeping daughter, aware that I would not be able to pick her up like this for very much longer. I carried her into the house. All the trees and fallen leaves were wet. Sheila opened the door. I didn't take Sonia up to bed. I carried her into our living room, dropped her gently on the couch, and turned on the TV. Sheila, confused by my haste and abstraction, said "What are you doing?!"

The moment I turned on the television, and I am not making this up, I saw Robin Ventura swing and send the ball, with the bases loaded, over the center field fence. The wet, tired Shea crowd exploded. My mouth simply dropped open. I didn't want to wake Sonia. My wife, thank God, seemed more mystified than pissed off. I saw Todd Pratt turn to hug Robin and I wondered if he could do that. I saw what looked like somebody being called out and I screeched, even though Sonia was sleeping. But the announcers explained that the run counted, but all four wouldn't, that the hug had reduced the grand slam to a single, because technically one runner had passed another on the base paths. I felt bad for Robin. But the Mets had won the ballgame. They had won. They should win the playoffs now. I was so happy, in the late night Connecticut quiet, as my daughter slept, and as my wife waited for all the commotion to be over so she could ask me how the day had been.

The Mets and *Frequency*

In the winter between the 1999 and 2000 seasons, a film called *Frequency* was released, starring Dennis Quaid and Jim Caviezel. It was about a man named John Sullivan who finds an old ham radio set in his closet that had belonged to his father Frank, a New York City fireman who died fighting a fire on the day the Mets won the second game of the 1969 World Series. The premise of the film is that something happens with sunspots that enables John to talk to Frank, with the ham radio, across the space of thirty years. This miracle allows him to tell his father how to avoid dying in the fire. It also allows him to work with his father to prevent the murder of his mother, which would have been an accidental consequence of saving his father's life. Ultimately, it allows John to get Frank to quit smoking, so that Frank is able to live long enough to be able to show up at the house in 1999 to save John from the guy who murdered some women and would have murdered John's mother if John and Frank hadn't prevented it. The reunion of father and son at the end of the film is very moving but technically it isn't a reunion because, in the revised reality made possible by the sunspots and the ham radio, the father has been around for John's whole life, and at the end of the film, John can remember having had his father for his whole life, even if at the beginning of the film, he has a crippling emptiness in his life and soul caused by the fact that he lost his father in 1969 at the age of 6, and therefore never learned how to ride a bike or live successfully.

It is difficult to conceive of a more implausible premise for a film. But somehow, when I watch *Frequency*, I never feel like reproaching the film for its implausibility. One reason for this is the excellence of the acting. Another reason is that when I watch *Frequency*, I don't actually experience it as a film about time travel or solving murders or anything like that. To me, it is a film about being a baseball fan and about being a member of a family.

The Sullivans are Mets fans. They are iconic Mets fans. They live in Queens, where the mother is a nurse, the father is a fireman, and the son will become a cop. They work hard and they live in a neat, humble, and lovely little house on a quintessential Queens street lined with such houses. They are part of an ethnically and racially diverse community of people who live as they do, who play softball in Mets caps and shirts under the Triboro Bridge, and who gather together to watch the 1969 World Series. As a child, John, whom his father calls "Little Chief," always wears a Mets hat and a Mets shirt and the son and father have a bedtime ritual of singing "Take Me Out to the Ballgame." Throughout the film, it is John's ability to tell Frank what is going to happen in each game of the 1969 World Series that makes it possible for the characters to realize that the miracle they are experiencing is "really" happening.

It isn't possible to talk to your dead father. It isn't possible to bring your father back to life after he's died. As I and others who have had loved ones with Alzheimer's know, it is sometimes not possible to ever again talk to your dead father even before he's dead. When people die, you lose them. Maybe there's a heaven where you will see them again and maybe there isn't. But there are no miracles that will return anyone to life.

Miracles can be imagined, but what is the good of that? Anything can be imagined. There is nothing miraculous about a miracle that happens in a novel or a film or a daydream. There can, however, be something miraculous about what happens in a baseball game or a baseball season. This is as close as we get. Miracles can't happen. But baseball miracles, which aren't really miracles but feel like miracles, give us a sense in our gut that they could.

If the people who made *Frequency* just needed some way for John to prove that he was really in the future, they could have chosen anything. They could have set the film in July of 1969, during the moon landing, and have John tell the father what Neil Armstrong would say when he stepped on the moon. But that wouldn't have been the same. The story of the 1969 Mets works as the emotional core of the film because it suggests that it might be possible to have what you know perfectly well you cannot have.

Just as baseball gives us a sense of the plausibility of miracles, it also gives us a particularly sharp awareness of how easily anything can be other than it is. Mike Scioscia swings his bat one quarter of an inch lower and his ball is caught at the wall and 1988 is different for millions. One close pitch by Kenny Rogers is called a strike instead of a ball and 1999 is different for millions. There is a hair's-breadth difference between life and death, horror and happiness. Baseball appeals to us by intensifying our awareness of this tiny border crack. *Frequency* does this too. The film focuses on the tiny difference between what is and what might have been. It offers a dream of reversing an accident that has left us on the wrong side of the crack. Baseball fans understand the appeal of this. Everybody does.

I fall for *Frequency* in the same way I fall for baseball. It moves me deeply, even though the more I think about it, the more uncertain I am that it deserves to have the effect it has on me. On a shelf in my room, when I was a kid, I had the same Mets bobble-head doll that Little Chief has on his shelf. Like Little Chief, I wore Mets hats and Mets shirts every day and I had a sense that rooting for the Mets connected me with my (now dead) father and with everyone else in my family. But when I am honest with myself, I find that I don't really have a clear sense of the degree to which baseball connects me with anyone. I know that I watched the sixth game of the 1986 playoffs with my family, and the sixth game of the 1999 NLCS. I know that we've gone to all these games together but what does any of this mean? We just sat in the same room or the same block of seats and we were happy or nervous or sad at the same time.

You know, sometimes when I feel that baseball is claiming to be something important and deep in my life, I feel the impulse to deny it. I think of all the ways in which it falls short, as a human experience. It gives people a sense that they share an emotional involvement, but it may just be substituting for other and more satisfying kinds of intimacy. It gives people a sense that they are part of a community, but it may just be filling the deep well of loneliness with something that is considerably less than friendship. It may just fill time, and lives, that might be better off filled with something else. At some level I am horrified by the hold this thing has on the souls of millions of people.

But if I believed all the rational arguments I make against baseball, my life would be very different. And *Frequency* wouldn't move me as much. But it does move me. I am so happy that John got his father back and my eyes fill with tears when I see the reunited family in Mets caps playing softball under the Triboro Bridge, when John hits the ball far and drives home his father, as his little son, in the same Piazza shirt my daughter has, runs out to run alongside the living, graying grandfather plucked from death.

2000

The 2000 season inevitably began with the resolution that what happened in 1999 should not happen again. Three good seasons in a row had to lead to something. So, knowing that starting pitching was one of their few weak areas, the Mets signed Mike Hampton, one of the best pitchers in baseball. John Olerud was lost as a free agent to Seattle, his home town, which really hurt, but the Mets brought in Todd Zeile, who was as bright and as steady as Olerud, if not quite as talented. We still had a great infield. We still had the best hitting catcher ever to play the game. The Mets should have been better than they were the year before. And Atlanta couldn't really keep this thing up, could they? The Braves had won every Eastern Division title since they had come into the Eastern Division of the National League. Their dominance had to end at some point. And if it was going to end, surely the Mets would be the team to end it.

The Mets won the National League pennant in 2000. Given that we did not in fact dislodge Atlanta from the top of the standings in the Eastern division and given what happened after our dramatic spectacular playoff victories over St. Louis and San Francisco, I sometimes have to remind myself of this fact. 2000 was one of the best and most exciting years in Mets history, but I don't think I need to tell any other Mets fan why, in the end, in memory, it doesn't really feel that way.

The good part is that once again we had this wonderful team of sympathetic and interesting ballplayers. The great 1999 team was still there, except for Olerud, and a few pitchers who had been replaced by others who were just as good or better.

In 2000, we had the same exciting rivalry with Atlanta, which had been intensified by John Rocker making the stupid mistake of telling a *Sports Illustrated* reporter that he hated our city for some of the reasons that most of us loved it.

We also had the big distracting dustup with Roger Clemens allegedly throwing at Mike Piazza. Years later I have to admit that I don't think Clemens actually meant to throw at Piazza's head, but at the time I have to admit that I enjoyed thinking that he did, and I hated him for it.

So we had our heroes and our villains and our big successful season. We didn't beat Atlanta, but we won the Wild Card with room to spare. We won 94 games. We were nothing to sneeze at, and in the playoffs, we decisively and dramatically beat the Giants and the Cardinals, who were both, that year, incredibly good teams. The Giants and the Cardinals, and the Mets, truth be told, were much better teams than the Yankees in 2000. The Yankees only won 87 games, and sort of stumbled into their division title, losing fifteen of their last eighteen games but winning it anyway when the Red Sox did whatever it is that the Red Sox will do, when it has to do with the Yankees.

What happened next should be one of the greatest baseball memories of my life. I had always dreamed of the Mets facing the Yankees in the World Series. My dream had come true. But it was a nightmare. It is still a nightmare. And you can't wake up from it because it all ended a while ago. This is one of the joys and miseries of baseball fandom. What has happened is always there. The good and the bad. You have it forever. Or almost. Sometimes something happens that can change the meaning or the feeling of what has happened. Though sometimes the meaning or feeling can never be changed. Sometimes the sour thing just hangs and never changes until everybody who remembers it dies and it can be forgotten. Sometimes I see ancient baseball statistics and standings and think that these numbers refer to things that once meant a lot to a lot of people. Now they mean nothing more than hieroglyphics on tablets.

I wish I could forget the Subway Series of 2000. I wish it was already in the oblivion it will be in a hundred years from now. But it is possible that there will be another Met-Yankee Subway Series during my lifetime, a Series that could change the meaning and even possibly the memory of the first one. It is also possible that I won't see another Subway Series, and what is in my memory will be as it is for the rest of my life. Or maybe there will be another Subway Series and the Yankees will win it and that will make everything even worse.

The sickening thing is that it really would have been very easy for everything about that Series to have been entirely different. This is always the case with everything that happens in baseball, but with this series, it really was spectacularly the case.

The first game was exciting. The first two runs were scored by the Yankees in the sixth inning, but then we had a three run seventh and led 3–2 going into the bottom of the ninth. But Armando Benitez gave up a walk, two singles and a sacrifice fly and the Yankees had tied it. The game was almost randomly decided by a single by Jose Vizcaino in the bottom of the twelfth.

The second game began with the overhyped insanity of Roger Clemens unaccountably throwing a piece of Mike Piazza's broken bat right back at him, thinking, or so he said, that the jagged oblong piece of wood was a baseball. Knowing that he only meant to throw a very strange baseball and not a dangerous piece of wood at Piazza, Clemens was able to continue pitching with a clear conscience. Obviously this gifted and unpleasant man knew how to work himself into some kind of hormonal trance in order to pitch at his best. He was absolutely astonishing for eight innings. I have seen many well-pitched ballgames, but I honestly don't think I've ever seen a more formidable or intimidating pitching performance than what Clemens turned in during the first eight innings of the second game of the 2000 Series.

The Yankees were up 6–0 going into the ninth. But once again the corpse staggered out of the grave, the thing at the carnival popped up out of the hole. Mike Piazza hit a two-run almost foul home run and the Mets ended up scoring five runs in the ninth. Amazing. But not six. Not seven. The Mets had played reasonably well, but they were down two games to nothing. Well, what more appropriate culmination could there be to this absurd era of Mets history than a spectacular comeback against the Yankees in the World Series?

Our comeback began as we won Game 3, 4–2. And we almost won Game 4, 4–3. Through four games the Yankees had scored one more run than we had and they were up three games to one. But the comeback narrative was still plausible. The Series would go seven games, I reasoned. It had been fated to go seven games.

In the fifth game, Leiter faced Pettitte. Leiter was beautiful and all that the Yankees could manage was two solo home runs, by Bernie Williams and Derek Jeter. Pettitte, though, was his postseason self. The rhythm and personality of this Series had also been set. Everything would be close and painfully hopeful and hopeless. The score was 2–2 going into the ninth inning at Shea.

Leiter struck out Tino Martinez and Paul O'Neill to start the ninth.

He had thrown about 140 pitches. But he would not leave, and Valentine was letting him stay in. Valentine had guts. If he was wrong, people would second-guess him forever. But I felt at that moment and I feel now that Valentine was right. Leiter had to stay. The Mets at the turn of the millennium were Leiter and Piazza. You had to go with them. You had to let them be the ones to say when they didn't have it any more. They might not be right, but they had earned the right to call it. Besides, who were you going to bring in? We had two really good relievers, but in situations like this, it seemed as if you couldn't trust either of them. I didn't want Benitez. I didn't want Franco. I wanted Leiter. All of us wanted Leiter. We would have wanted him even if he had already thrown 200 pitches.

Posada got a hit and Brosius got a hit. Little hits, nothing that could be read as a sign of Leiter's collapse. Luis Sojo, a defensive replacement inserted in the eighth inning was coming to the plate. That wasn't too scary, was it? He hit something up the middle that maybe should have been fielded. But it wasn't. Jay Payton fielded it in center and threw the ball perfectly to home plate. Piazza could have caught the ball. Posada would have been out. But the perfect strike to home plate hit Posada on the thigh and bounced into the Yankees dugout. Both Posada and Brosius scored.

The Mets still had one final turn at bat. With two outs, and Benny Agbayani on first, Mike Piazza hit the ball with his short lightning swing. This should have been the tying run. It was hit well and far, but in the deepest part of center field, Bernie Williams caught it against the fence.

The Series was over. Every moment of it had been excruciatingly close. Everything that happened in it was on the verge of being something entirely different. But the closeness of the individual games would be beside the point. You knew that this would go down as a five-game series, decisively won by a dominant team that had accomplished the impossible task, in the contemporary era of baseball, of winning three World Championships in a row. We Mets fans who lived through this knew that this Yankee team wasn't dominant. This wasn't the extraordinarily beautiful and balanced Yankee team of 1998. This team wasn't nearly as good a team as the Braves. We knew what no one would remember: that the Mets were actually better than the Yankees in 2000. But we could sit in the stands at Shea at the end of that fifth game and think whatever we wanted to think. Everyone had already gone home.

If, after a bad lunch, or on a crummy afternoon, somebody in an office in 1976 had decided not to accept either me or my wife into the same graduate school, every single thing in my entire life would be different. If my mother, in 1948, had gotten wind of the fact that her brother, inviting her to dinner, was trying to set her up with the man who became my father, I would not be right here right now, banging away at my laptop and you would not be doing what you're doing at this moment. A week or two after the World Series, the year 2000 was to offer a much more dramatic example than the Subway Series of how random fortune is, of how close things can come to being entirely different. Sometimes the razor's edge of fortune gives you something you might not deserve. Sometimes, with everything on the line, it leaves you with something you desperately do not want to have. There has never been any way around the fact that this is how reality works. This is the primal joy and pain, the unavoidable central fact of existence. But baseball is not reality. It is optional. Sometimes you wonder why you do this to yourself.

2001

On August 28, 2001, the Mets were ten games under .500. They were approaching the end of an unhappy baseball season and they seemed to have no hope of catching the Atlanta Braves, who were not themselves having a great season but who were still about 10 games ahead of the Mets.

Something turned around as the Mets headed into the last month of the season. The Mets won 10 out of their next 12 games before Al Qaeda terrorists hijacked four planes, slammed two of them into the towers of the World Trade Center, one into the Pentagon, and one into a field in Pennsylvania. About 3000 people were killed, most of them New Yorkers in the World Trade Center. For the first time in major league baseball history, play was suspended during a regular baseball season. When it resumed on September 17, the Mets streak continued, with a desperate, impossible fierceness that brought all Mets fans to their feet. Excited Mets fans called WFAN to share the dream of a historic elevation from ashes, only to be ridiculed by the relentless false and irrelevant rationalism of Mike and the Mad Dog.

The first baseball game played in New York after September 11 was played at Shea Stadium on September 21, 2001, against the Braves, of all teams. All the players wore NYPD and FDNY hats and after Diana Ross sang the National Anthem, the Mets and the Braves embraced on the field, to demonstrate that the worst baseball animosities were still a form of friendship. The Mets won the game, on a home run by Mike Piazza. They were only 4½ games behind Atlanta. They would win 8 out of 9 games after September 11. They would win 18 of the 21 games they played between August 29 and September 27. Then they dropped two decisive and heartbreaking games to Atlanta and ended up losing 6 out of their last 9. If they had won the 6 games they lost, they would have tied the Braves for the Division Title. I know that this isn't really coming close, but it is more than anyone could have anticipated at the end of August. And it would have been one of the best baseball stories ever. And it really felt, during that inconceivably horrible September, as if it just might happen.

It didn't happen, but I won't ever forget how it almost did. I don't care what Mike and the Mad Dog said. It almost did.

The Yankees, of course, won their division and Yankee fans got very sentimental about this. It wasn't just Yankee fans. In the aftermath of 9/11, a nation that had for so long despised New York was, in the wake of our disaster, trying to find ways to embrace it. The new identity that was emerging for New York was exaggeratedly positive and its dominant image was that of the heroic policemen and firemen, who had gone into the buildings to save others, and who were now cleaning up the horrible mess. I was pleased that this new image was emerging for New York. But I had problems with the way in which some Yankee fans and out-of-towners were trying to connect this image to the New York Yankees.

If the Mets had pulled it out, I reasoned, it would have been okay to connect heroic 9/11 New York to the Mets. Miracles are achievements of the spirit that are considered miraculous precisely because they happen so rarely. A fourth consecutive World Championship is not a miracle, by definition.

A Red Sox fan (!) told me that he was rooting for the Yankees to win the World Series because poor New York needed something to be happy about. Gently but firmly, on behalf of my city, I am afraid that I spurned his generous sentiment. New York needed the world's love and support. But it was never necessary to root for the Yankees to win for any reason. And so when the Arizona Diamondbacks deprived the Yankees of their fourth consecutive World Championship in the seventh game of the World Series and the Yankee fans began to talk about how broken-hearted they were not to win it, IN THIS PARTICULAR YEAR, you don't even want to know what I was thinking.

I'm not going to tell you that I'm proud of this. I'm just telling you what I felt, as a Mets fan.

The Mets at the Beginning of the Millennium

The exciting Mets team that spanned the millennia never won anything after 2000. Between 1997 and 2001, the Mets had two very good years, two great years, and one mediocre year with an exciting finish. The Mets won the Wild Card twice and the pennant once. They did not win a division title and they did not win a World Series. But they had been fun and good and, in a limited way, triumphant. This was the third good era of Mets history. But like all good eras in the history of the Mets, these five seasons would be a complicated memory, with a sour tang of disappointment mixed into the lingering sweetness.

The good times should have lasted longer. Yet when the roller coaster plunged in 2002, and rattled along the bottom for three years, we were disappointed but not surprised. This had happened before. And while it was happening this time, it was hard to point a finger and get angry. Later, people would point their fingers at Steve Phillips and get really angry, but I have to admit that nothing he did between 2002 and 2004 seemed really stupid to me at the time. I never liked the excessive dependence on veterans in the Phillips era, because I like to root for a team that has at least some youth. But if the idea was to win and win soon, because Piazza and Leiter wouldn't last much longer, it seemed to me that most of Phillips's moves made a kind of sense.

I mean, who could argue with the acquisition of the great Roberto Alomar? Wasn't it reasonable to think that the 26 home runs Mo Vaughn hit for us in 2003 were not all he had left? Who would have thought that Jeromy Burnitz could actually get into a slump at the start of a season and never get out of it? Who would have thought, in 2000, that Rey Ordonez and Edgardo Alfonzo would not actually turn out to be superstars for the new millennium? Who knew that Armando Benitez, one of the best Mets closers ever and that is saying a lot, would develop this weird tick of only blowing the games that mattered the most? Who could have guessed that Kaz Matsui, with his sweet, vulnerable smile and his rave references, was only just barely good enough to play in the major leagues? I wish they hadn't traded Scott Kazmir for Victor Zambrano, but I would be lying if I said that the trade didn't make at least some sense to me at the time it was made.

We knew that Franco would eventually lose what he had left after so many years of pitching. We knew Piazza would eventually lose his ability to catch any base stealers at all. We knew that Al Leiter would not be able to give us his smart, steady seasons forever. I guess what happened is that the core of our great end-of-the-millennium team aged as you would have expected, and the guys who were supposed to take their place just didn't happen. And so we had three seasons of mediocrity and disappointment. We had become a bad team again, which was hard to understand, because every spring it looked as if we might be good.

Maybe this was Steve Phillips's fault and maybe it wasn't. I really don't know. It was always hard to tell what kind of job Steve was doing because he talked like a politician's press spokesman. He could talk his way out of anything. Oh, he would still be fired when the results weren't any good, but if you just heard his interviews, you might easily be convinced that he couldn't possibly have done anything wrong. Maybe he did do something wrong. Maybe he didn't. I still don't know.

When you're a fan, you spend a lot of your time second-guessing the decisions of the people who make them. But you always know that you're not close enough to the action to have any right to second-guess. You give management credit for their successes, but if you disagree with a player move, you feel vindicated by its failure. This isn't really fair. How do you know what you would have done if you had all of the information about Vaughn, Burnitz, Matsui, Ordonez, or Alfonzo that Phillips had? Often things work out as they do because of good or bad luck. Have you ever watched the players up close in practice? Do you actually know them as human beings? Have you ever discussed things with the doctors or the scouts? Do you ever have any legitimate reason to think whatever you think about any of them? No. So what good are your speculations, your guesses from the far distant sidelines? They're as good as your judgment when you yell at the umpire when you want a ball and he sees a strike and it kind of looks like a ball to you from the upper deck and he's behind the plate. You don't know anything. You are just imagining things.

That doesn't mean that you should just shut up and trust their wisdom. You know that they might not deserve your trust. But what are you supposed to do instead of trusting them? You want to trust them. You don't want to despise them, because that would interfere with your ability to love the team they create. To me, as a fan, owners and the front office are a couple of the fingers on the hand of fate. They are involved in a part of baseball that I can't see and never feel I know. They do stuff, and when the season opens, there is the team, and I embrace the team. Even if the front office has done a bad job, I embrace the team. What do I know? I embrace the team. I would not accept this condition of dumb passivity in any other aspect of my life. But I accept it when it comes to the Mets. Why write about a condition as debased as this? Maybe there is nothing beautiful about it. Maybe I am just an idiot. I'm not trying to be funny or coy when I say this. Sometimes I really think this.

As the Yankees continued to win and the Mets continued to disappoint, the Wilpons finally fired Phillips and brought in Omar Minaya to replace him. Omar was not like Steve Phillips. He was upbeat without appearing to spin. He was confident in a way that made you hopeful. I liked the way he talked, with his Queens accent with Spanish edges. He didn't sound like anyone else. Not only did he not remind you of Steve Phillips, he didn't remind you of any general manager you had ever seen before. He was neither beefy nor geeky. He was serene, and he had dash. He put you in mind of Oscar de la Renta. He had close-cropped white hair and he looked great in a polo shirt. There was something astonishing about what he had accomplished, without resources, to improve the Expos. Who knew what he would be able to accomplish with resources? Omar was different and he was on to something. I liked him. He filled me with hope. He had the name, the smile, and the style of a magician.

2005

Heading into the 2005 season, Minaya and the Wilpons did three things right away to bring the Mets back to plausibility. They signed Pedro Martinez and Carlos Beltran. And they hired Willie Randolph to be the manager.

When Willie Randolph was hired, I had mixed feelings. Former Yankees have to prove to me that they are Mets, according to my own idiosyncratic definition. As oddball eccentrics, Stengel and Berra were Mets right away. It seemed as if they had been proto–Mets all along. They certainly didn't seem to have been formed in the immaculate Yankee mold.

I knew that Randolph was from Brooklyn and that he grew up a Mets fan, and those were points in his favor. But I was immediately ticked off by his Yankee-style rules about facial hair. I happen to have a lot of facial hair and I resented the implication that it might get in the way of anyone's ability to maintain a professional appearance. And that no drinks on the plane rule? It's as if the Mets organization had never gotten over that ignominious flight from Houston to New York in 1986. Some players and wives got drunk and some seats on the plane were broken in celebration of winning a National League pennant. Can't have something like that happen again!

But that was twenty years ago. Nobody hells around like that anymore, even when they win the pennant. It's not in the culture. If anybody nowadays acts like an ordinary baseball player from the decades before 1990, the press is on it right away and the offending party guy is getting professional help by the end of the week.

Still, in spite of his puritanical Yankee rules, Willy Randolph won me over pretty quickly. I began to see the rules thing as a mild and gentle way of establishing a sense of structure. I saw the effect Willie had on the players, in 2005 and particularly in 2006. He reminded me a little of Gil Hodges. He was calm, but in a controlled and not in a tranquil sort of way. Like Hodges, he could come across as a little stern. And like Hodges, he inspired tremendous loyalty in his players. They knew that he was on their side, and they also knew that he wouldn't let them get away with anything.

A lot of people criticize Willie because sometimes he makes decisions that no one can justify if they only examine the evidence and are only willing to respect the powers of human reason. Willie respects his own imagination, and he has the courage to believe that it might help him in his work. There is something particularly beautiful about a managerial decision that springs from a creative apprehension of what a ballplayer might be capable of in a given moment. Willie makes this kind of decision a lot and the radio waves and the Internet rumble whenever he does. Willie does not believe that managing a baseball team is an exact science. He thinks it's more like a social science. Hell, sometimes it looks to me as if he thinks it is like writing poetry. In 2005, the Mets won twelve more games than they won in 2004. In 2006 they won fourteen more games than they won in 2005. I know that there are lots of reasons for this. But I am convinced that one of the reasons is Willie.

In the 2005 season, Pedro Martinez thrived and Carlos Beltran faltered. Cliff Floyd surprised everyone with a spectacular year free of injuries. Cliff was such a great guy, and I rooted so hard for him from the time he first came to the Mets. It was such a vindication to see him play so well, to see him having the kind of year everyone always thought he could have. Mike Cameron was also wonderful, a superb and eager outfielder with power who was shoved over by the Beltran signing. Still, he was always so happy to be with us, and he continued to give us everything we could ever have asked from him, just as he had when he hit 30 home runs to no avail in 2004.

How wonderful it would have been if Cliff Floyd and Mike Cameron could have led us to the right conclusion of the Piazza era, to something that could have redeemed the three bad years after 2001. Piazza was no longer what he had been, but he still was plenty. In 2005, David Wright developed into a superstar and Jose Reyes moved far enough in that direction to keep us from getting too impatient. 2005 was a sort of breakout year, but a series of strange events kept the Mets from winning the seven extra games they would have needed to make it into the postseason. There was the fluky 0–5 start. There was the titanic collision of Floyd and Cameron that knocked Cameron out for most of the rest of the year. The biggest thing, however, was the Beltran mystery or rather, non-mystery. The main thing that kept us from the Wild Card in 2005 was a painfully shy man's stage fright after signing an immense contract to play for many years in the biggest city in the United States.

All year long, the team hung around .500, waiting for Beltran to wake up. At the end of August, the Mets looked as if they might be ready to charge up the humble little hill of the Wild Card. There was a good feeling on the team. It had too many holes to be a great team, but it was filled with spunk and promise. The Mets were about to play their first meaningful games in September in a long time. And they did. But the meaning wasn't good. The Mets disappeared down a hole of a road trip and lost 14 out of 17 games. They lifted their heads for a push in the final week, just so that they could plant their flag on the right side of .500.

And so in the end, the corpse of this first good-feeling season in five years had to be laid bitterly on the heap, with the other disappointing seasons of the twenty-first century.

Mike Piazza

At the end of the 2005 season, the Mets did not re-sign Mike Piazza. You had the sense that Omar Minaya wanted him to go, as he had wanted Leiter to leave the year before. This had been Mike Piazza's team and it could not be any longer. It had to be something different now.

More than any Mets player except Seaver, Piazza had created and defined an entire era of Mets history. He lifted an exciting but wobbly team to the point where it thought that it was as good as the Braves and destined to beat the Yankees in the World Series. The team wasn't as good as that, but Mike was great enough to allow us the pleasure of the illusion. He had a glamour and an explosive talent that was like nothing we'd seen since the Eighties. I will always cherish the fact that for seven years, I got to watch the career of one of the best right-handed hitters since DiMaggio, the best hitting catcher in history.

Piazza was a gentle and modest superstar. His skills were enormous, but he seemed to stand in the background behind them, like a parent, expecting you to look at them and not him. Sure he knew you were also looking at him. How could you not? He was handsome and perfectly formed and he stood more firmly on the ground than anyone else. But he looked as if he had no interest in being a star. He was only interested in smacking the ball where it needed to go, and controlling the game from behind the plate with his steady force and will.

In more than forty years of watching baseball, I don't think I've seen anything as beautiful as Piazza's short miracle of a swing. It made no physical sense. It was too short to send a ball that far, but like a swift, silent explosion, it did. When Piazza came to the plate you leaned forward to see the swing. You kept your eyes focused on the spot where his arms and the bat would be and you prepared yourself to see the split second of contact and to shift your gaze to the long path of the ball's flight. You got ready to stand. On every pitch. If it didn't come, you didn't mind because you knew it would come soon. And when it came, you felt yourself seeing and remembering it at the same time, because you knew you were watching something rare and unique and that once he could no longer do it, you would never see anything exactly like it again.

I loved to watch Piazza catch. I loved the energetic confidence of his crouch, and the surprising speed of his springing up after foul pops. I loved how he would stand on the mound with his mask off and everyone would look straight at him, as if he were the captain, the main guy, the only one who could make things right. His arm, as everyone knows, was not as strong as a catcher's arm needed to be. And as he got older, he didn't throw out many runners. Yet one of the things I liked most about watching Piazza play was seeing his face after he failed to throw a runner out. He had that sad, determined grimace, a twitch of his closed mouth, with his eyes focused straight ahead. He wasn't surprised, but he wasn't resigned. When he did throw out a runner, he looked pleased, but he also looked as if he knew that next time he probably wouldn't.

Maybe it was vain of Mike to catch for so long. But I was glad he got the catcher's home run record. He was even better than Bench and Fisk and it was good to mark that with a number. I thought it was inspiring that Mike was so devoted to the craft of catching that he wouldn't let it go. He revered his work and he wanted all of the catchers in the future to know that he had been there. Playing his position near the end, Mike was as eager and as hopeful as a rookie. But he was a thoughtful grown up who could not fool himself. His dignified disappointment wasn't always a happy thing to watch, but it was as much worth seeing as his home runs.

The fans loved him, without any reservations. At Shea, you'd see and you will see forever the number 31 on bent backs and little backs, on broad backs and narrow backs. No one should ever wear that number in that uniform on our field again. He won us all over, with his bat and his heart and the beauty of his play.

Mike gave us the great years of 1999 and 2000. And he gave us the

GOING TO THE GAME WITH MY DAUGHTER

small spasms of hope we had in the years after that. He was one of the greatest players ever. And he grew older. He'd get bunged up, and he'd be out of the lineup, and he couldn't lift the team any longer. I wish we had held those one-run leads in the bottom of the eighth and tenth innings of the sixth game of the 1999 Championship series against Atlanta. I wish we had shown the Yankees something to fear in the 2000 World Series. Just three or four games tilting the other way would have given the Piazza era a more satisfying flavor in the memory. But it was fine as it was, and by 2005, it was time to move on.

Going to the Game with My Daughter

Whenever I go to a Mets game with my daughter, we arrive an hour and a half before the scheduled first pitch. Not an hour. Not two hours. An hour and a half. It's funny how, with every person with whom you go to a game, there are specific rituals and specific rules. When I meet other people to go to a game, it's not an hour and a half. With my daughter it is always an hour and a half.

Arriving an hour and a half before a game, we can choose where to park our car. The stadium lot has more cars in it than you might think, but it is not crowded yet. We park in a space that is close enough to an exit that will lead us easily back to the Whitestone Bridge, that doesn't have any visible signs of glass, broken or otherwise, that is not too close to some guys playing catch, and not too close to anyone cooking hot dogs on a hibachi. We park so that we can just drive forward and don't have to back up to get out.

We get out of the car and walk to our entrance. We usually enter through gate "B" because although our seats are normally closest to "C," we get to "B" first and we like to get into the stadium as soon as we can, because as long as we are outside of the stadium, we are outside of the

— 114 —

stadium. I always buy my tickets online now and we always get Loge Reserved as close to home plate as possible.

My daughter offers her bag to be searched and we do the thing where the cheerful stadium security people wave the wands around us. I don't understand why my watch, wallet, keys, and shoes will always make a metal detector at an airport go off but they never make one of those wands do anything different. So be it.

We present our printed-out tickets to the old guys who take the tickets. They look like the same old guys who took the tickets when I was a kid, but they're not. We go into the stadium, and then depending upon what we have negotiated in advance, we either visit the Mets store or we do not. If we don't, and we normally don't, we go right to the kosher hot dog stand near section 9 on the Loge level. We're not kosher, but these are the best hot dogs you can get in the stadium. They are absolutely incredible, real, all-beef, kosher deli hot dogs. I get two hot dogs with sauerkraut and a potato knish. She gets a hot dog with nothing on it and a knish. We get one of those big Diet Pepsis to share. Then we go and get ketchup and napkins. She likes ketchup on her hot dogs, to my infinite chagrin. I should mention that my daughter is now a vegetarian, and she's rather strict about it. But this ritual of us getting kosher hot dogs at the Met game goes back many years. It is the only exception my daughter makes to her vegetarianism, and she makes it with a real seriousness. Many things are important in life, but some things must take precedence over other things.

We take our food to our seat, and set up the Diet Pepsi in a place of honor so that it will not spill. She handles the delicate business of getting the ketchup on her hot dog without getting it all over her. I transfer the sauerkraut from the little plastic bowls to my hot dog. And once we have everything where it should be, where it will not spill and make a mess, we start to eat and we watch and we enjoy being in the stadium an hour before the game will start.

We talk. And we always have things to talk about even though we have just spent an hour and a half talking in the car as we drove down. Our talks on the drive down are wonderful. We expect to talk, as we've always talked on these rides, about serious things. As soon as we get into the car in Connecticut, we are ready for our serious conversation and we have it and it lasts until we get within sight of Shea. As soon as we see the stadium from the Whitestone Expressway, we are there, and that conversation we were having reaches a natural end. When we get inside the stadium, the topic shifts to baseball. As we eat our kosher baseball lunch or supper in the stands, we talk about how much we love baseball and how much we love the Mets and how cool and bright the stadium looks. We usually go at night, because both my daughter and I are complete and total suckers for the way the stadium looks at night. We watch the crowd come in. We watch the opposing team finish up batting practice. We make comments about people. We see and hear the planes overhead. We pay a kind of desultory attention to whatever pre-game ceremonies or awards or performances or events they have. And when we're long done with the food, with the unfinished gigantic Diet Pepsi tucked way back under my seat so that it will not get knocked over if I have to suddenly jump up, it is finally time for the National Anthem. We enjoy our sense of being Americans at a baseball game. She always comments on how the anthem has been performed. She takes voice lessons and her great dream is to someday sing the Star Spangled Banner before a game at Shea. We sit down and the game begins.

My daughter welcomes each Met to the plate with a genuinely loud high-pitched non-verbal holler, that you also hear a magnified version of any time a Met does something really good. She is totally into the game and she knows all the players and has her own very positive sense of their skills and their character. Don't tell her I told you this, but she really isn't that much of a fan. At least not in the way I was at her age and still am. She is completely indifferent to statistics and she never watches or listens to a game unless I am. If there's a game on and there's a rerun of *Queer Eye for the Straight Guy*, she will choose *Queer Eye* every time. But when she is watching the game with me, she is totally into it. I think she thinks that paying attention to the Mets is an important link she has with me. She is already very sentimental about the fact that we've gone to all of these games together. I can't help but think of how the number of games I will go to with just her, when she's still at home in our house, is pretty small. It can probably be counted on the fingers of two hands. This makes all the time we share at the stadium enormously valuable and meaningful. But it happens in real time and it is such a fun thing to do, you don't want to get too maudlin about it. It would ruin the experience.

I also think my daughter does baseball on her own terms. Fine. She's really into drama and it seems to me as if she experiences the game as if it were a dramatic production. She likes the tense moments, the amazing things that are done, the way the individual players' characters show through in what they do. She loves to cheer and applaud. She loves the stuff on the Diamond Vision. She always cheers wildly for our section color in the plane or car race, even though she knows that I think it is stupid. She has an uncanny ability to actually pick which hat has the baseball under it at the end of the shell game. She stands and waves her hands for the t-shirts. She wishes there were more human waves. I wish there were less. She looks for and is very happy when she sees Cow-Bell Man. She always shouts "Lets Go Mets" when she is prompted to do so.

We have so much fun. Even when they lose. Even if the game is absolutely terrible. Don't tell the Mets, but normally when my daughter and I go to a game a Shea, they lose, and often something really disastrous happens. When they win, though, and you get to go down the ramps in a really happy crowd, there's nothing like it. We get to the car as soon as we can. We nose out slowly, letting people walk by us, being charitable to cars trying to get into our line. We get onto the Whitestone Expressway. She knows and I know that we now have another memory and that nothing lasts forever. If she has energy we'll make up stupid songs and do the kind of dumb and repetitive improvised comic routines that my wife is glad to know we share with each other but definitely doesn't want to be around to hear. If she's tired, she'll sleep. And I'll just sit and soak in my happiness, coming back from a ballgame with my wonderful daughter on a quiet highway with the dashboard lights and the hum of the car.

The Crowd at Shea

When I take my seat at Shea, I see every kind of person around me.

I see the couple from Astoria with charcoal dark hair and metal in their ears and noses, rooting for the team without any of the irony you might expect them to have. I see Dominicans, proud in polo shirts, holding Dominican flags because they are so pleased that everyone knows that Pedro is such a great pitcher, and Omar is such a great general manager. I see Irish and Italian and Jewish families from Long Island who have rooted for the Mets since the very beginning, whose grandfathers played stickball in the streets of Brooklyn.

I see the bald guy bracketed by his grandsons, the wary fans of the other team, the old couples like married bears, the somber family all with the same face who open up a box with a store-bought cake and sing "Happy Birthday."

How brightly lit and vivid are these faces of people you will never see again! Near me are some people speaking German, some computer guys talking shop, an intense young woman with a very big camera, some old men in very old hats, two ultra-orthodox women in long jeans skirts and bright orange Mets shirts, men with moustaches and thick wedding rings and their arms around their kiddies and their wives.

Looking over the tops of the heads, I see cornrows, spiked hair, pony tails, and yarmulkes. I see lawyers in bedraggled business suits, men who look like busts of Roman emperors, and kids who cannot believe their good fortune, to be here, to see the game, to buy all the food and the flags and the foam fingers. Many of the guys are barely presentable, like guys, but most of the girls have taken the trouble to look nice, no matter how casually they're dressed. All races mix, all cultures and ages gather, here in a broad mass of blue, black, and orange flecked with pink, yellow, and white. Above us growling from time to time, are lumbering planes with lights like jewels. Weaving or waddling through us are the vendors, in their fluorescent yellow-green t-shirts, with metal boxes on their heads or with trays of trembling sodas. They are the flight attendants in our giant spaceship.

I love how you see a rapid ripple in the crowd, as people rise to catch a foul. I love how the crowd is like a giant baby. It can't speak, but it can make broad noises of content, excitement, dismay, and dissatisfaction. It is a loud crowd, here at Shea. It is a powerful thing when stirred. The Mets know we're here. The Mets drink from us. They always have and they always will. Sometimes it scares them and sometimes it helps them do things no other team ever does.

In the big crowd at Shea, I love the sense that all these people from different places and different worlds have come for the same reason I have. Most of what we choose to watch pushes us deeper into our individuality. Baseball, in the open air, draws us out. It gives us a rest from our uniqueness. It gives us a brief and valuable sense of what we have in common with others. In the generous glow of the game, you look around and see reflections of your past, present, and future, in all the little clusters of families, children, teenage friends, old people. You see Ellis Island decades later, plus all the migrations that came before and after. You marvel at the fact that everyone has found their way to this place, and to this quintessentially American way of enjoying being alive.

I am with everybody in this crowd. I am with all the people who have loved the Mets in their first five decades, and all the people who will love them in the future. Mets fans of the future, you should know that I too knew the despair of the division title lost in the final week, the blow of the home run by the opposing catcher that slits the throat of hope in a sickening second. But I have also known what it's like when the bases are loaded and the clean-up hitter swings his bat swiftly and the ball goes up so high and to the right and I can't see it, but I know it is going far, and I look for the white speck in the brilliant black sky, to see if it will leave the park. I know in a moment like this that I am feeling exactly what thousands of other people are feeling. Like everyone else in the stands, or by their TV or radio, I feel the rush of the grand slam. I think of seeing all those runs on the scoreboard, and I jump up to shout and scream. At a moment like this, I am connected to everyone around me and I am connected with you. You will see something like this. You will have this, too.

Diamond Vision

I've come to like Diamond Vision, or whatever they now call the two screens that show digital video, one on the scoreboard, and one in a box at the top of a tower to the left of the scoreboard. I hated the first, more primitive version of Diamond Vision. I felt that it replaced the organ and I had loved the organ. The organ made you feel as if it was the 1920s and you were at a silent movie. You were. What you saw was all there was. And all you heard were the sounds of the crowd, and the organ, which was all there was to coach you to cheer the hero and boo the villain.

When Diamond Vision came, in the eighties, it seemed to me as if somebody had plunked a giant TV on stilts next to the scoreboard, for the sake of younger fans who couldn't be happy with the corny, peanuts-and-crackerjack sound of the organ, who wanted something more contemporary than Jane Jarvis playing "The Teddy Bear's Picnic" to entertain them between innings. I liked "The Teddy Bear's Picnic." I was a fan of Jane Jarvis. I liked the fact that being at a baseball game was so different from watching it on TV.

But this was a resentment that wasn't worth feeling. Diamond Vision has been around now for more than twenty years and at this point it is as much a part of the experience of Shea as anything else. The newer generations of fans, people like my daughter, cannot imagine a game without it.

The Diamond Vision lets you know, first of all, when the game is finally about to begin, by giving you the kind of New York-y jazz and lights introduction you get before shows like *Saturday Night Live* or *David Letterman*. A sense of occasion is created by the neat images and effects, like a Mets insignia revolving in a blue field filled with floodlights. After the first half-inning, the Diamond Vision tells you what you can and cannot do at the stadium, in highly Latinate English ("moderate your consumption of alcohol," "please refrain from using inappropriate language") that is probably not clearly understood by potential abusers.

When play begins, the Diamond Vision is helpful and informative. You see a picture of a player and you can make cracks about his facial expression. You see his stats.

The main use of Diamond Vision, however, is to entertain the crowd between innings. People who would have, in the past, stared abstractedly at the planes while listening to "The Teddy Bear's Picnic" now get to follow the bouncing Mr. Met head and sing the original "Meet the Mets" song. Or they get to see a pleased but befuddled family upgraded to luxury seats, or they learn that "rookie" is "novato" in Spanish from Professor Reyes, or they use their knowledge of world landmarks to determine "Where in the World is Mr. Met?" or they root with puzzlingly genuine enthusiasm for the color of their seat level as virtual planes or pizza trucks race to a virtual finish line.

One thing I like about Diamond Vision is that it increases your sense of the crowd of which you are a part. You identify with the upgraded family, or the people who have to answer questions about 1980s pop music or identify the meanings of very hard vocabulary words. You like to see people preening for the Smile Cam. My favorite is the Kiss Cam. I like to see people just sitting there and suddenly realizing that thousands of people are looking at them and want them to kiss. Sometimes they're stunned, sometimes they're amused, and sometimes they're embarrassed. Sometimes they peck, sometimes they turn red and don't do anything, and sometimes they smack their faces together with a flourish. I love it. And the roll call of people and groups "The Mets Welcome" is always touching and sweetly banal and interesting. Those are definitely real people's names, having birthdays and anniversaries. Those are the real names of groups, offices, organizations, clubs. Investment offices, trucking companies, cooking clubs, school groups. Everyone has come down to meet the Mets! Everyone is here. The Diamond Vision welcomes them.

So, you see, I can get used to new things. I welcome all the novelties. I'm not going to be one of these old fart baseball fans stuck in his nostalgic prejudices. As long as there is a link with the past, I am happy. And there is a link with the past on the Diamond Vision. There is that cozy, corny tone that has been for almost half a century the style of the

New York Mets. That goofy, ironic, family feeling. That blue-collar good humor; street-smart, cynical, and incomprehensibly optimistic. That whatever, what-the-hell, silliness. That, who us? a great baseball team? Huh? That we wanna be good we wanna be good but hey, what just happened? That we are the champions, we are the champions, oh no!, Mets thing. Think about it, fellow morons. Only two moments of pure, unmitigated triumph in 45 years. But that's not why we're here, is it?

The Home Run Apple

At Shea, every time a Met hits a home run, a big wooden apple, with a lit-up Mets logo on its breast, rises slowly out of a great big black hat in center field. When the logo has flashed a few times, the apple descends back into the hat. Mets fans love this. It's wonderful.

Why an apple? Why a hat? Well, at some point in the late sixties, for some reason that isn't entirely clear to me, the Mayor's Office or somebody decided that it was time to start calling New York City the Big Apple. To the best of my knowledge no one had ever called it this before. It was unclear to me and presumably to many others why New York suddenly needed a cute nickname, but perhaps they thought it would be helpful to have one, and a ready-made logo, for a publicity campaign to boost tourism. I think we were told at some point that this was actually old jazz musician's slang for the city. Usually, I think, jazz musician's slang is pretty cool. In this case, perhaps, it isn't. Calling something an apple conjures images of classrooms with inkwells and appreciated teachers. Apples are cute and corny. They don't really work as a symbol of New York City. And it is too easy to make a joke about rottenness.

But all of these considerations didn't, in the end, make any difference. The apple became a symbol of New York. And shortly after this happened, I think it was in the seventies, as baseball teams were inventing all kinds of mascots and home run celebration ceremonies to try to attract people to the ballpark, the Mets built a big hat, a big apple, and some sort of primitive elevation apparatus, and put it out in centerfield to entertain us.

It was pretty lame. But as the history of Mets public relations illustrates, what seems lame when it happens soon becomes fun, and then beloved, and then indispensable, and finally iconic. We love the apple. We love to see it come out of the hat. It is so strange and beautiful. It is better than fireworks, which are too obvious. It's almost as if the apple, with the glowing logo, is some kind of Cyclops, or Loch Ness monster, that is awakened when the ball clears the fences and we cheer. Its silence is so much of its charm. It is also big. And there is nothing like it anywhere else. Where else does an apple come out of a hat? We've got the only one.

We've been promised that the apple will cross the parking lot and assume its place of honor in the new stadium. It'd better be the old one. It better not be updated. Nobody wants an animatronic computerized new kind of apple. We want the old thing the way a kid wants his old Teddy Bear and not some unsmelly new one. We will need the old apple to remind us of old Shea, a place that was happy to be tacky, because baseball games were once carnivals. They weren't media events. They weren't slick. The apple will be the embarrassing relative who is always threatening to fart in the living room. The apple will stand for the last century. Even the people in the luxury boxes will want this.

Cow-Bell Man

There is a man called "Cow-Bell Man" who is perfectly self-explanatory. He is a fan who comes to what seems like every game and walks through every level of the stands banging on a cow bell. He has made himself as much of a beloved feature of Shea as the apple. He reminds older fans of Karl Ehrhardt, the Sign Man, who could be found at almost every game in the late sixties and seventies and who held up signs to comment on whatever was happening. Sign Man used words.

Cow-Bell Man uses rhythms. Though to be honest, the rhythm of his beating of the cow bell is always pretty much the same. It encourages you to cheer the Mets and Cow-Bell Man. When people hear him they look around and there he is. Everybody seems very happy, although sometimes people on the Internet complain that he is annoying. What? He's making too much noise?

Cow-Bell Man is like everyone's personal celebrity. Everyone has seen him. Often, and close up. You can't miss him. He bangs a cow bell and he wears a Mets jersey that says "Cow-Bell Man." You go through your whole life without actually seeing most celebrities. Or if you see a celebrity, they are far away or on some kind of stage. The Mets are celebrities and you have seen them often. But you are rarely if ever close to them and even if you are sitting in the best seats in the house, you watch them across a barrier.

Cow-Bell Man is on our side of the barrier. Several people have told me that they have seen him going to the game with his family on the number 7 train. He says hello to everybody in the car of the train. He'll smile at you if you cheer him at the stadium. What celebrity is this accessible? What celebrity can become this familiar? Hey, how often do you see Mr. Met up close if you don't sit in the field-level seats? Cow-Bell Man is an ordinary man. He is one of us. Yet all of us know him. He has escaped anonymity. We know that there are millions of Mets fans because we have seen hundreds of thousands of them with our own eyes in the stadium. Yet how many Mets fans can we name? We can name our friends and families and Jerry Seinfeld and Tim Robbins and Jon Stewart and Cow-Bell Man and Doris from Rego Park. That is enough of a reason to become Cow-Bell Man.

Why aren't there more stadium characters? What is to stop somebody from walking around blowing a horn and calling himself Horn Man? What is to stop somebody from wearing a gigantic Mets hat and calling himself Hat Man? Or Woman? It is funny how few of us will take fame on these terms. But I am very glad that someone is willing to go to every game and bang a cowbell. It's nice to point to somebody you don't know but you see a lot and say, that person is a Mets fan, a famous Mets fan, famous for being a Mets fan and not for something else. Cow-Bell

Man has earned the right to stand for all of us, even if all he does is bang a cow bell.

Seventh-Inning Stretch

Every time seventh-inning stretch comes around, you realize that it always comes at just the right time. You are ready to stand up, and you are ready for a mental break in the action, before you get into what is normally the most emotionally absorbing part of the game. At Shea, people stand up for "Take Me Out to the Ballgame," with the words appearing in an illustrative cartoon on the Diamond Vision. At Shea, and maybe at other stadiums, everyone sings the song and many people do a kind of upper-body standing dance that has developed to its rhythm. People aren't even conscious of the fact that they know how to do this dance. But if you watch, you will see that a lot of people know it.

If you think about it, you realize that you know it yourself. It starts as you lurch your head to the left with the first "Take." Then "Me" has no beat and your head is just in the middle. Then everybody lurches to the right with "Out." Then you move your head back through the middle with "To The." Then it's lurch to the left with "Ball," and then you immediately lurch right with "Game." The pattern is different with the next line. To the left again with "Take" and then a slow soft glide from left to right with "Me Out To The," and then a right lurch with "Crowd." The third line, "Buy Me Some Peanuts and Crackerjacks," just has people moving their head back and forth from left to right, without any lurching. Then, for emphasis, they tilt their heads back on "I" and "Never" as they sing the line "I Don't Care if I Never Get Back." People then tip their brows down and forward with a rolling motion as they sing "Oh It's..." This is so that they can jerk their heads back up again for the first, most vigorous "Root," which is followed by jerky little nods for the next two "Roots." Then some people sing "for the hooome team" and some people sing "for the Meh-ehts." Then people move in any way they want for the line "If they don't win, it's a shame." The last line: "And it's one, two, three strikes you're out, at the old ball game" is also pretty much free form as long as you do something demonstrative with your head or arms for "one, two, three." This is the way it's done.

At Shea, as soon as "Take Me Out to the Ballgame" ends, you immediately hear the loud bouncing rhythms of an Italian song called "Lazy Mary," sung mainly in Italian in a recording from the 1950s by someone named Lou Monte. You hear cries of pleasure and encouragement as if everyone were waiting for the song. Everyone knows this song, but few people actually know what it's called. If you ask people to identify it, you'll get answers ranging from "The Tarantella" to "Crazy Mary," and most people think that the singer is Louis Prima, who Lou Monte sort of sounds like. The song is sung at Connie Corleone's wedding in the opening scene of *The Godfather, Part I*. In *Godfather, Part II*, Frank Pintangelo tries to get the Nevada orchestra playing at Anthony Corleone's First Communion party to play it and it comes out, to everyone's dismay, as "Pop Goes the Weasel." The rhythm is like that of "Pop Goes the Weasel," but the song has a lot more character and for generations of Met fans, it sounds like some kind of celebratory affirmation of New York ethnicity. Just as Lenny Bruce once said that everyone in New York is kind of Jewish (he was referring to their ironic sense of humor and a tendency to rhetorical complaint), there is this unspoken sense, when New Yorkers celebrate something, that everyone in New York is kind of Italian. In any event, everyone claps and bounces up and down to "Lazy Mary" and everyone always looks as if, bouncing and clapping to this song, with all these other people, they are having the time of their lives.

Then "Lazy Mary" ends, there is the usual milling around, and the stretch is officially over when the announcer on the loud speaker says "Now batting for the New York Mets, number...." It's as if it all hadn't happened, but people are still amused that it did.

The Guys Who Wipe the Seats

There are these guys who wipe off the seats for you at Shea. I suppose they're officially called ushers. They stand guard in the sections of the stands behind or near home plate. You don't see them in the less desirable seats at the ends of the horseshoe. If you can't manage to sneak past them, they will confront you and ask to see your tickets. This is a pain if you're carrying food. But you play along, as if you were going to a Broadway show and needed to get your Playbill. Once they look at your ticket, they lead you to the seat and vigorously wipe it off with a towel they've used to wipe off many other seats. They do this even if your seat is dry and clean. I give them a dollar or two, depending on the size of my party. I thank them loudly and sincerely.

They know that you would just as soon not deal with them. They know that they're not strictly necessary. They're local, no nonsense guys with grey hair and bellies. They try to look at people who don't tip them as if they're the kind of people who don't know how to do anything. And they have an overplayed dignity. They don't want you to think that they are like the guys who try to clean your windshield.

Who are these men and why do they put up with the indignity of wiping the seats of people who may or may not want their seats wiped? They can't make very much money in tips and I doubt they are paid much of a salary. This can't be anyone's full-time job, eighty-one times a year for just a few hours. They see people dodging them and looking past them. They stand waiting for tips that may or may not come. But I don't pity them. These guys get to go to every game. They work at Shea. They are always there. From the looks of them, they've been there a long time. They are part of the whole thing. We envy them their crappy work. We would do their job. Hell, we would clean up the peanut shells, and the beer bottles, and the boxes and the wrappers. We would clean the goddamn toilets.

What would it be like to be part of it? To not pay to enter the stadium? To draw a small salary from the same bank account as the players? To stand and face the crowd, with the lights on your back?

Curtain Calls

At Shea, when a player has hit an important home run, he is expected to return to the dugout to slap or poke or punch the hands of his teammates. As he does this, the crowd stands and claps and calls the player's name. After a suitable interval, the player steps out onto the top step of the dugout and takes his hat off to the fans. We call this a curtain call. Other teams hate this and newspapers in other towns have wasted a lot of ink decrying it. It has been called the height of New York arrogance. The Mets and Met fans are accused of "showing up" the opposing pitcher and team. When new players join the Mets, someone tells them that whatever they may have thought of this custom in the past, they must now do it honor. They cannot refuse to come out and raise their caps. With this gesture, they must show that they know that the Met fans love them and are grateful for what they have done.

This is not New York arrogance. In New York, many of us go to theatres and opera houses, where this admittedly unusual custom originated. Met fans long ago noted that there is an analogy between a home run and a bravura performance. When Broadway shows, or the Metropolitan Opera, go on tour to cities like Atlanta, St. Louis, and Cincinnati, does everyone stop clapping as soon as the performers have finished taking their bows? Is it considered inappropriate for the audience to clap and shout after the curtain has fallen, in an effort to compel the performers to show themselves one more time? If there are such rules governing audience behavior in other cities, I will take this into account when I visit them. In New York, the custom is different.

Those who do not like the custom of curtain calls say that they insult the other team. No insult is intended. If someone on an opposing team hits a home run, it does not mean that you are worthless. You can hit home runs against them. Why should you care if the fans of the other team wish to express their appreciation? Does it surprise you that they are happy and grateful? Did you not know for whom they were rooting? If they cheer very loudly, and if the player tips his cap, will they have taken an unfair advantage? Will they have hurt your feelings? I sincerely hope not.

As a Mets fan, let me say that we will not mind if your players take curtain calls in your stadiums. We will be glad to see that your fans like you as much as we like the Mets. Please don't worry about showing us up. Enjoy yourselves. Let your fans enjoy themselves. Let everyone have the pleasure of saluting the performers. Let everyone enjoy, for as long as they can, the afterglow of a great performance.

Booing

I hate it when some Mets fans boo a Met. You can boo players on other teams. That is not booing. That isn't personal. That doesn't hurt. That is just part of the fun. When you boo your own guy, you are trying to hurt him. Don't give me any crap about how you boo people to make them perform better. Booing doesn't have that kind of effect on people.

I hated what was done to poor, sad, humble, thinly talented Kaz Matsui. It's not his fault that he was signed, that he was given a job he couldn't handle. I hated it when Carlos Beltran was booed in 2005, because he had signed a big contract and had a mediocre year and was struggling too hard to adjust. I hated it when Jeromy Burnitz was booed. He was so sunny faced and so California and he had such a weird looking, bad looking swing. It became a thing to boo him when he couldn't get his average above .210. Did the booing help? Let's say some Mets fans hadn't booed Burnitz. Has it occurred to you that he might actually have been able to get out of his season-long slump?

I really hated it when Armando Benitez was booed. I know he was arrogant and childish and blew some big games. But he was an amazing relief pitcher. He closed most games down with ease, as you watched the scoreboard to see if he would hit 100 mph. Closers should never be booed. When anyone else on a team has a bad game, you hardly notice. When a closer has a bad game, the team loses. Yet closers have bad games too. Closers have slumps. And they have a terrific record of going bad and then becoming good again. Their work is a mystery. And booing fouls them up.

My hatred of booing Mets goes way back. I hated it when George Foster was booed. I was disappointed in him too, but I knew the booing wouldn't help him get better. I hated it when Doug Sisk was booed. He fell out of a decent groove. If a guy gets out of his groove, booing can convince him that he never had a groove to begin with.

The players are normally very gracious about being booed. They say something grown-up about New York fans having high expectations and that those high expectations are a challenge that they welcome. Bullshit. Their feelings are hurt. The booing means that we want them to go away, not that we want them to get better. When their feelings are hurt, when they feel we don't want them, they find it hard to relax. They press too hard, they can't find their stride. In the rare cases when a player does get better, they get better in spite of the fact that they've been booed. Booing is mean and ungracious. We should be kind and encouraging to all of the Mets all of the time.

Others will disagree. They will argue that the booing of disappointments is part of the particular intensity with which Mets fans cheer the successes of their team. New Yorkers, they argue, can't help being demonstrative. They can't keep their mouths shut for merely logical or tactical reasons. I still argue differently. What I like most about New Yorkers and Mets fans is that they are sentimental and hopeful. They want out-of-towners and less intense people to feel at home in New York. They take great pride when a player whom everyone thought wouldn't like the city ends up liking it. They are proud of their city and they want its greatness and warmth and tolerance to be appreciated. We have the Statue of Liberty, for God's sake. We are the golden door. We welcome and absorb anyone and everyone. We don't want to put down the people who stumble when they first come. We don't hate failures in this town. We love underdogs and comeback stories. We want even the wretched, if well-paid, refuse to know that we are behind them, that we want them to get up again.

I never boo a Met (unless he says something really awful about the Mets or Mets fans). And that's not because I am an unusual New Yorker. It's because not booing your own guy when he's down is part of my idea of what it means to be a New Yorker. To boo, to me, shows an impatience that is incompatible with being a Met fan. Booers have lost hope. They're calling for the hook. They've stopped the story and the breath of the game, because they no longer believe in the possibility of a surprise. And if you don't expect surprises, if you don't live for surprises, you shouldn't root for the Mets.

The Mets in Queens

As I love the stadium, I love the spot on which it stands, in spite of the winds and the noise of the planes. It makes sense that Shea is so close to LaGuardia and Kennedy. It's a place that takes you on a journey.

Shea is built on the Valley of Ashes. It is exactly where George Wilson's gas station would have been. Though it's built on the landfill from incinerator ash, it isn't a vacant or dreary place. It is a beautiful place, with beautiful summer sunsets. Great things have been done or created near here. From his house in Corona, Louis Armstrong walked to games at Shea. Walt Whitman taught school over the centerfield fence in Flushing. As I amble down the concrete ramps at the end of the game, and see Manhattan off to the west glittering in the thick night air, I think of how right across Roosevelt Avenue, in a workshop under the El, Louis Comfort Tiffany made his lamps.

Queens knows it is not the famous part of New York. It is not Manhattan. It is not even Brooklyn. But it is as much New York as they are. Most of its houses date from the time between the wars, as the other boroughs overflowed. There are thousands of rows of little twenties houses. There are English Tudor neighborhoods from the thirties. There is a chain of impossibly exotic yet quaintly American downtowns, connected and separate, some not even a mile apart.

Sometimes I park my car in a public lot in Flushing, in the Asian neighborhood that spreads out under the green tower behind the U-Haul sign. You can get better Asian food here than you can get in Manhattan. And then you can walk across the bridge to the game. Sometimes I drive down Roosevelt Avenue, under the elevated tracks of the No. 7 train. I pass Colombian-Ecuadorian restaurants, Himalayan restaurants serving Indian, Chinese, Tibetan, and Nepalese food. I pass Argentine nightclubs and Middle Eastern all-you-can-eat buffets. In the speckled light under the El, dodging double-parked cars and vans, I feel like I am spinning a globe. What I eat, and the world I will enter, will depend on where I find a parking space.

Queens is one of the most interesting places in the world. It doesn't just have individuals from everywhere. It has communities from everywhere. If you were looking for the most representative 70 square miles on the planet, here is where you would find it. John Rocker, the hated relief pitcher for the Braves, noticed this during the great Mets-Braves rivalries of the late '90s. And when he stupidly observed to a reporter that what you saw as you rode the No. 7 train might not be American, we jumped on him. He fell into our trap. Part of the idea of Queens, and the idea of New York, is that loving America may mean having to love the whole world that ends up in America. He didn't think of that. Idealistically, and somewhat disingenuously, we made it out as if rooting for the Mets was what that was all about.

Queens is a world's fair. And Corona Park was home to two of the most famous ones. The glamorous 1939 Fair was here, with the Trilon and the Perisphere. Here was my 1964–5 Fair, beside the new Mets stadium. A few times I have parked my car in the park, near the Unisphere and the crumbling New York State Pavilion. I love this strange evening ghostland. Among the ruins, I remember the optimistic fountains of more than forty years ago, shooting into the sky, surrounded by arcs of futuristic concrete lit by green and cobalt footlights.

When I lived in Astoria, a Greek neighborhood a mile to the west of Shea, I saw that everybody in Queens roots for the Mets. Almost everybody. More than anything else, the Mets give an identity to Queens, which is so diverse and so relatively new that it resists having an identity. When you walk past the travel agencies and the lawyers' offices and the stores that sell phone cards and fruit for much less than what you pay in the suburbs, you see all the Mets caps and jerseys. You see the Mets flags draped from the iron balconies on the two story buildings on the little streets crowded with trees and old people in lawn chairs. You see that the Mets are to Queens what the Red Sox are to New England. The team unifies and reflects the place. And when the Mets are really good, Queens doesn't feel like an outer borough. It feels like the center of the world.

I know that I am not really getting to know the world's people by coming to Queens. I know I am just eating their food and enjoying their storefront displays and their signs. I know this as I know that when I sit in the big crowd at Shea, surrounded by all kinds of people, I am just enjoying the impression of all their differences. But I like Shea, and I like Queens, and I liked the World's Fair because I like to see that there are things, like cities and fairs and games, that bring so many different kinds of people together.

It is forty-two years since we came back to our car in the World's Fair parking lot at 11 pm and the Mets-Giants doubleheader that began at 1 pm was still on the radio. It is still the longest doubleheader ever played. We are now in the World of Tomorrow. The World of Tomorrow looks more like Main Street, Flushing, or 94th Street in Corona, or Steinway Street in Astoria, or Roosevelt Avenue in Jackson Heights, than it looks like the City of the Future in the General Motors Pavilion. But the Mets are still here. And they're still the Mets. They're still in Queens. And Queens is still Queens.

Inside Bob Murphy's Voice

Everything is fair and safe and well-intentioned. The bases are firmly anchored and the weather is perfect. People have funny stories to tell about each other.

I am happy in the back seat of a car on a dark road because Joe Christopher is coming to the plate. It is early March, but spring is here. I know whether the ball that has just left the bat will leave the park, and if I don't know, then it will be very close and very exciting.

I might have been lonely on a long drive, but I'm not, because an old friend is with me. An uncle, really. Except not as much of a pain in the ass as my real uncles.

I know it is good to be a parent, a husband, and a friend. I doubt that those who do bad things really mean to do them. I am glad when the Mets win, but I have sympathy for the misfortunes of others.

Young kids are eager and veterans are wise. The young kids will become veterans. The veterans will retire, but they won't die for a long time, and you will still run into them from time to time.

Everyone has something interesting to say. Every bad thing that happens can be borne. I am awake and full of hope.

Afternoons are pleasant in prospect. Nights are evenings. They are to be enjoyed. It is never morning, but somehow it always seems to be.

It is 2 A.M. in my dark upstairs bedroom and it is the twentieth inning and neither the Mets nor the Astros have scored a run. One summer in my thirties, almost all the recaps are happy. A man I have known all my life dies when I am almost fifty and I never wrote him the letter I always meant to write him, telling him how much he meant to me.

Inside Bob Murphy's voice, I am glad to be on the earth. And I am one of the nicest guys you could ever hope to meet.

Ralph Kiner

The old Mets' TV post-game show, *Kiner's Corner*, would begin, remember, with music that sounded like something a German band would play at an Oktoberfest. It was the wrong kind of music for a show like this, but hey, it was Ralph's show and Ralph was Ralph and it was all right for that reason. When the music faded, you'd see Ralph sitting in a chair, with that way he had of looking like he was completely at home and yet had just been beamed down from Mars and was still getting his bearings. A ballplayer would be in the other chair. Ralph didn't seem completely aware of why the ballplayer was there but he recognized that it was his obligation to make the player feel comfortable. So Ralph would ask a question at the end of which you could not possibly justify putting a question mark. The player would listen and then, when he finally realized that the question mark was not coming, he would start talking. He would usually say something about expecting a fastball because the pitcher had thrown him a curve ball on the two previous pitches and it was a fastball and high and inside and he got a piece of it and he was glad that whatever happened happened.

Ralph, without betraying or expressing his emotions in any way, would always wait until the player stopped talking before he began asking his next question. The player, who knew this time that a question mark was not coming, just as he had known that the curveball was not coming, was now more at ease and he would launch right into his next disquisition about the pitch he expected and the pitches the pitcher threw and blah blah blah. After Ralph did this three or four more times, the show would end and you would hear the bratwurst music again.

It was a great show. There was something hypnotic about it. I don't think Ralph was on the sauce, as some have suggested. But I also don't think he hosted *Kiner's Korner* the way he did on purpose. Lindsey Nelson and Bob Murphy did and said what they did on purpose. Ralph just happened. That was his charm.

A lot of times Ralph would open his mouth and words would just fall out of them. Fathers on Fathers' Day were all wished a Happy Birthday. Current ballplayers would briefly borrow the names of ballplayers who hadn't played for thirty years. And we would learn things like the fact that the Mets had a good road record when they played at Dodger Stadium.

Still, as funny as he could be, Ralph isn't and wasn't a comic figure. He has presence. He is the guy who comes along, who sits in the back seat and doesn't call attention to himself. You talk with him a little to be polite and you find out, always to your amazement, that he was one of the greatest home run hitters who ever lived, that he knew everyone who ever played, that he has a deep, inner knowledge of the workings of the game, and that he's slept with half of the women who still get you excited in great American films of the 1950s. What are you supposed to make of an existence like Ralph Kiner's? How could someone hit all those home runs, know so much about baseball, sleep with Ava Gardner, and still be Ralph Kiner? Quick, imagine Ava Gardner on *Kiner's Korner*. Something close to this may have actually happened. And all you can do is imagine it. He remembers it. I think. Imagine what Ralph Kiner's memories must look like.

After a while, you realize that this humble, relaxed man really is who he says he is. You realize how smart and witty he is, without apparent effort or even intention. You end up loving him, and needing him to be there, but you still don't know where to put him. You can understand why you loved Bob Murphy because he was a great announcer and he had his uniquely generous and hopeful view of the universe. Lindsey Nelson, with his thirties voice and seventies jackets, was an accomplished showman. Gary Cohen and Howie Rose are the new style of great announcers, articulate professionals. What is Ralph? He's just somebody you couldn't have made up and you've come to love. He is like the soul of old baseball, from a time when people were characters and life was an adventure, even for those who weren't adventurous. As Ralph slips away, I know I am losing something. I still want to hear his voice, even with the palsy. I can still understand him. I need to continue to know that his world really existed.

Ralph threw out the first pitch at the second NLDS playoff game in 2006. I saw him from my seat way up in the upper deck. He had on a bright yellow sweater. But even at that enormous distance, you could tell it was Ralph. You could tell by the way he ambled, by how big and solid his head and his body were. There he was, so far away and so familiar. Throwing the ball to the catcher. Sort of. And then walking off the field.

Howie Rose

I've always had a real affection for Howie Rose, ever since 1987, when he began to host *Mets Extra*, a three-hour pre-game show on WFAN. Three hours of *Mets Extra* was extra, all right. *Mets Extra* is now just 40 minutes. The original show was overkill, but it was just what I wanted. During those great years in the middle of the '80s, I could have listened to five hours of *Mets Extra*. I could have listened to ten hours.

Howie was the perfect host for the long version of *Mets Extra* for the same reasons that I like him so much to this day. He is not a jock. He is like me. Howie always says that he has a face made for radio. I don't know if that's true, but I know that if I was a captain of a baseball team and was choosing up sides, I'd look at him and pick him last. He's never faced a 90-mile-an-hour fastball, but that's okay because facing a 90 mile-an-hour fastball will not teach you everything there is to know about the game. Howie is one of us, but that's not to say that he's a regular Joe. He's not. And he's not trying to be. You won't get any of the bullshit macho from Howie. There's some subtlety to the way in which he understands the universe, both the baseball one and the other one.

Howie's not ashamed to use big words. but he never sounds pretentious when he does. He uses them as if they were part of the English language, and so why wouldn't you use them? He uses them for fun, when they're not really necessary. When a foul ball is hit into the dugout and scatters the players, he'll talk about the ball upsetting the "previously sedentary Dodgers." He'll talk about a pitcher who gets bombed as having had an outing that was "anything but unscathed." If an outfielder catches a ball, after having a little trouble finding it, Howie will say he caught the ball, "but not without some angst." And then after he says something like this, he won't ever say it again. It won't become a catch-phrase. Howie doesn't speak in formulas. Like any truly articulate person, he uses the language with pleasure, and you never know exactly what he is going to say when something happens.

Howie's amazingly smart, but he's no snob and he loves baseball passionately and he knows that loving the game so much doesn't require him to be an idiot. Quite the contrary. Howie represents those of us who are always going to be kids in dark, poster-cluttered upstairs bedrooms secretly listening, at midnight on a school night, to the West Coast game on a little radio. Howie represents those of us who keep scorecards and know batting averages and really do know how many games the Mets won in each and every year of their existence. Who but someone like Howie could, for hours on end, keep up a Mets conversation worth listening to (notice I said "worth listening to").

I like how Howie can get annoyed. It's good to have a baseball analyst or announcer who can call crap for what it is, who can say, like Howie says, "Oh come on..." This is something that Bob Murphy, whom I loved and will always miss, could not do on the air. In Murph's world, people could not be called out for their crap. He might say "my, my" or "what a shame," but he wouldn't do what Howie does. Howie will complain, forthrightly, about what should be complained about. One of my favorite Howie moments was in 1988 when Tom Seaver's "41" was being retired and Seaver was being driven onto the field as the fans cheered and the stadium announcer began to describe the special car in which Seaver was riding, which had obviously been provided to advertise the manufacturer. Instead of playing along and saying how great a moment this was, Howie was livid. As the stadium announcer was going on and on about the car, Howie said what the fans were thinking: "Everybody's got to get in a plug. Everybody's got to get in a plug. They can't just let this moment be what it should be." I don't remember his exact words. It was something like this. I remember Howie's on-target outrage and I remember how glad I was that he was screwing up the moment the sponsor had paid for.

It's all in his name, Howie. He's not Howard. He doesn't have the perfect resonant radio voice that Gary Cohen has. His voice is a little nasal, a little whiny. He's just as articulate as Cohen, which is saying an awful lot. But he talks like your cousin Howie who got into Harvard. Unlike Gary Cohen, and sort of like Steve Somers, Howie still has a kind of old-fashioned Jewish thing going on in his voice. It's not a whole schtick like with Somers, but it's there. You hear it in the way he accents his words and alters his rhythms for maximum expository effect. This balances the New York Italian thing you get in the voices of Mike Francesa, Christopher Russo, and Joe Benigno. WFAN obviously likes to offer its diverse listenership this very little bit of ethnic flavor.

Howie also has what I, being Jewish, recognize as a certain Jewish rhetorical and pedagogical style. He's incredibly knowledgeable, he's generous with his knowledge, and he is really glad to be able to give you all of the benefit of his knowledge because you don't know nearly as much as he does. The Yiddish word for what Howie is is a "maven." There's no English equivalent to this word. It's a term of high praise in a culture that does not consider being a know-it-all to be an automatic strike against a person. Howie is a maven. He is the kind of authority who makes the world better by actually knowing what we all wish we knew.

Howie is so obviously the fulfillment of a fantasy. You can tell by looking at him and by listening to him that he probably always wanted to be a sports announcer. You can just imagine him in a basement in Bayside, with the TV sound off, calling the 1969 World Series. Now he gets to be a sports announcer. He gets to be friends with Ralph Kiner and Tom Seaver and Keith Hernandez and Ron Darling. He's not in the booth because he played, and so it's no surprise that he is better than they are at most of what's involved in the job they all do now. But he always knows that they are the stars and he is the fan. He's happy just to be there and we're happy with him and for him.

When Howie, in the middle of the '90s, made the switch from being an analyst to being an announcer, I remember wondering if he would be able to do it. Would he clog his play-by-play with too much analysis? Could someone so articulate and so ironic be sufficiently straightforward? I love the way Howie's become a great announcer, while still being a great analyst and still being Howie. He does all the usual announcer things. He sounds genuinely excited when the Mets do well. When he's excited, his words spread out, get louder, rise higher in pitch, to the point where he begins to sound like a carnival barker, talking loudly out of what seems to be the side of his mouth. He'll even do this carnival barker thing with some irony at very ordinary moments in the game: "And at the end of three..." ("Hit the bulls-eye with the baseball"), "And that ... takes care ... of the Mets" ("Get your tutti-frutti ice cream"). Like all announcers, Howie has a few trademark calls. When the Mets win he always says "Put it in the books!" or "Put that one in the books!" When a Met hits a home run, he'll often say "That's a goner!" When a Met makes a great defensive play, he'll sometimes say "Put a circle around that one!" But he uses his trademark phrases naturally. He never sounds like a trained seal, like the announcers for some other teams.

I hope I get to listen to Howie forever. I think he's exactly my age. Despite the rigors of the job, and all the travel, people who are lucky enough to get to be baseball announcers seem to want to do it until they literally no longer can. So Howie'll be working a lot longer than I will be. I'll listen to him when I'm retired. I'll envy him and enjoy him. And he and Gary Cohen will always be the sound of the Mets for my generation. I'll always love Bob Murphy and Ralph Kiner. They were dads, they helped me grow up. But Howie and Gary are my age. They're my buddies. And so is Eddie Coleman. I don't know Gary's brother Tom McCarthy well yet, but he seems like an awfully nice guy. He sounds just like Gary on the phone. But nobody sounds like Howie.

Listening to Mike and the Mad Dog as a Mets Fan

Let me say first that I like to listen to Mike and the Mad Dog. I enjoy the predictability and unpredictability of their show. There is always something new in sports and they talk about it and their callers call in about it and no one ever says anything that really surprises you. People play roles and fall into groups: those who think we ought to bench this player or trade for that player or sign this free agent, those who disagree, those who are in between, those who used to think one thing and now think another. There are the regular callers, obscure people who relish their stardom. There are the first-time (callers) long-time (listeners), obscure people with whom you identify, giddy with their long-anticipated moment. And in the middle of it all, there are Mike and Chris, like brothers, the bratty brother and the one who is supposed to be more responsible, with their half-real, half-cartoon personalities; half-adult, half-kid; talking with managers, players, and fans, living the fantasy of a million listeners driving home from jobs that are nowhere near as compelling as theirs. As in most families and groups of friends, the fun is just in the talk, in sharing the experience of following something you can't control. When you get into the rhythm of a radio show like this, you marvel at the waste of your time, but you enjoy the relaxing sense of being locked into something that is lively and familiar. I like this. I know where I am when I listen to Mike and the Mad Dog.

But however much I like listening to their program, I do not enjoy it as a Mets fan. Mike and Chris broadcast on WFAN, the Mets station, and millions of Mets fans listen to them and hundreds of Mets fans call them. But they get this wise-ass pleasure out of hating the Mets and rooting against them. I know it's part of the show, but I don't like it. Mike Francesa is a Yankee fan, all cocksure and pompous, and Chris Russo (called the Mad Dog because he talks funny and often pretends to be out of control with excitement or anger) is a Giants fan. San Francisco Giants. This is one of the great irrelevancies of life for sports fans in New York. We have to deal with and think about some guy rooting for a team that none of us care about. And we have to put up with it because they are Mike and the Mad Dog and people listen to them and I suppose they think they have some kind of rapport and can't be broken up. They couldn't find a Mets fan who could do that job?

Mike and Chris know a great deal about sports and they have amazing memories for what happened in individual games. But they have this absurd belief that their knowledge and perspicacity entitle them to make judgments about what is likely to happen in a baseball game or in a baseball season. They tell you that there is no way a team is going to win the three games that they need to win in a series in order to get into first place and then the team will win the three games. They will tell you that a trade is a bad trade in a tone of voice, and with an insistence, that suggests that they know that it is a bad trade and then it will turn out to be a good trade. Sure they're right more often than not, but they're not right that much more often than not.

Baseball is like this. Studying it is like studying political elections. It is not like studying physics. Sober, objective analysis will not pick you a winner much more often than flipping a coin. The whole point of being a fan is rooting for unlikely but perfectly possible outcomes. But you'd never know this if you listened to Mike and Chris who love to explain to Mets fans why there is no rational or legitimate basis for their hope and faith. Do they think that we don't know that Bennie Agbayani or Mike Jacobs are almost certainly not going to be Babe Ruths? Do they think that we don't know that the adrenalin boost after 9/11 is unlikely to lift the team above the mighty Braves? When it comes to Mets fans, Mike and Chris act like unhinged priests who have become the most cynical rationalists and are trampling on the simple piety of their parishioners. They don't understand Mets fans. They don't understand how what we want to do, on late summer afternoons in the middle of a winning streak, is gather our wild fantasies, bringing them together to ignite in a big ecstatic conflagration. We want the pleasure and the power of our improbable dreams. We don't want two guys with funny voices pissing on our bonfire.

We could live with it, perhaps, if they made their points just once. But this is a radio show, after all, and people are turning them on all through the show. So, if you are listening for more than an hour, you have to endure the familiar wavelike rhythm of a Mike and the Mad Dog schtick. An assertion stirs, gathers force, builds in intensity and then pounds the shore, only to recede, gather and build and strike again a short time later. Then it happens again, and again, and again, because all the callers waiting on the line are responding to the same goddamn thing. Normally a topic holds through an entire afternoon and nothing can dislodge it, until at some point, Mike and Chris just let it go without ever saying that they are letting it go.

As a Mets fan, I have the capacity to listen to endless repetition when what is being repeated has to do with the Mets and is interesting to me. But Mike and the Mad Dog have a knack for finding Mets topics in which I am not at all interested. For example, on Opening Day in 2006, they devoted their entire program to what they felt was the travesty of the Mets new reliever, Billy Wagner, using the same song to announce his entrance as Mariano Rivera has used for years with the Yankees. Oh my God! Over and over, we get told that you just don't do that (why?). Mariano is the greatest reliever ever (so what?). Everybody knows what song Mariano uses (they do?). The Mets and Yankees play in the same city (they do?). You can't use the same song if they play in the same city (you can't?). There is something really numbing about listening to this kind of thing over and over.

To prevent things from getting boring, Mike and Chris will sometimes take opposing sides of an issue. You can tell that at least one of them is just pretending. Usually it is the job of the Mad Dog to take what will be designated as the "crazy" position, so that Francesa can do his rational, authoritative, if only intermittently grammatical bit. It's funny, though, how I find myself agreeing with the Mad Dog more often than I agree with Mike. I think it's because his holy fool thing, his respect for his intuition, is more appealing to me as an approach to baseball than Mike's effort to come across as a wise man.

I don't know. I will keep listening to them. And I will keep getting annoyed. And I will just hope that the Mets will do something that Mike and Chris have said was impossible. And then I will listen to them give the Mets a lot of credit for doing it. I will hear them having to hand it to them. But they won't admit that they were wrong in a way that really means anything. They'll just admit that they were wrong in that "have to hand it to them" way.

Steve Somers

Steve Somers' voice is different from everyone else's. The first time you hear it, it is kind of disconcerting. It's as if you are listening to a puppet. It sort of bubbles up, getting louder and softer, higher and lower, with accents in unanticipated places. After a while, you get used to how strange it is and you start to like it. It can be hypnotic, even riveting. It's a nighttime voice, a voice that keeps you company when you're lonely, that soothes you when you're too nervous to sleep, by making you laugh but not so loud as to wake up the rest of the house. You have never heard it during the day and you can't imagine that you ever will.

Steve calls the Mets the Metropolitans, as if to say, "Who do they think they are?" "Who do we think we are?" "How can anyone really take them seriously?" "How could you not?" Somehow he seems to put an accent on every syllable of the high-faluting name. Without rushing it along. Leisurely. The Met-ro-pol-i-tans. Steve takes a one-syllable name and turns it into five. This is a good metaphor for what he does. Steve never says anything fewer than five times. You get the first version of the sentence. Then the second. And so on. By the time you get to the fifth, you get the point, and you have enjoyed the variations.

Steve expects you to enjoy repetition. One thing he'll do is give players nicknames with editorial content. Barry Bonds is always "Barroid" (Barry + steroids). This is a dig the first time you hear it. Not the cleverest thing you've ever heard, but okay. By the second or third time you've heard him say this, you've gotten the point. But Steve will never abandon his humble witticism. If you listen to him a lot, you will eventually hear him call Bonds "Barroid" for the thousandth time. And he will say it for the thousandth time with emphasis, as if you've never heard him say it before. This should be annoying, but somehow it isn't. Like I said, Steve is soothing.

I love how Steve seems amused that people call him, as if he is graciously surprised every evening to find that he is expected to host a radio talk show. He is infallibly charming to the first-time callers. And he treats his regulars as if they are his buddies. He also treats his hecklers as his buddies. Is there anyone he couldn't disarm? The first-timers are so excited that they praise Steve as if he is a god, which is just as amusing to Steve as the fact that they have called.

He is called the Schmooze. He schmoozes. I don't think there's any better word for what he does. He doesn't really talk. He analyzes, but casually and impressionistically. He is always being ironic, about the Mets, about language, and about himself. His intimate, self-mocking perform-ance is filled with pockets of real wisdom. But these always surprise you as much as they delight you, because you're never entirely sure if he's being serious.

Steve loves the Mets, and he loves them in the way they have to be loved. With exasperated affection. With befuddlement. With the kind of laughter that escapes as you breathe between your sobs. He doesn't like the Yankees or Steinbrenner. Neither do we. Steve is more like us than the ones in the afternoon. And he consoles us after they have spent the whole afternoon making fun of us.

Gary Cohen

What amazes me about the way in which Gary Cohen speaks is that there is never any hesitancy. Full sentences, short and clear and with pleasantly varied rhythms, come out of his mouth as if he were just unreel-ing something that has long been finished, polished, and complete. He always sounds perfectly relaxed and everything he has to say fits into the amount of time he has to say it. He is done with whatever he is saying right when it is time to turn his attention to something happening on the field. Or at least it seems that way. The game does not appear to interrupt his stories in the way that it interrupts the stories of every other announcer. There seem to be nothing but natural transitions between his analysis and his play-by-play.

Gary's voice is deep and beautiful. He sounds like a god who has gone to Columbia. It elevates, without losing its fluency, when a ball is put in play. And when something really big happens for the Mets, it climbs in pitch and in volume and it pulls you along with it into a zone of perfectly fluent excitement. The best example of this is the way in which he calls a home run. Gary has his famous trademark call: "IT'S OUTTA HERE!" but while a lesser announcer would put his main emphasis on getting to the call that makes you notice him, Gary is focused on the home run. Every home run gets its own unique build-up, as if it is an entirely unique event, with its own trajectory, its own level of suspense, its own significance. When you finally reach the release of "IT'S OUTTA HERE!" the phrase seems to be appropriate to that home run and that home run alone.

In Gary's voice, you feel that the game can always be encompassed and enclosed by words. Nothing is raw and unsayable. There is a comfort in Gary's authority. There is something soothing about his control. But the game stays as exciting as it should be. It has all of its power. It's not flattened out or smoothed out or dumbed down as it is by some announcers on some other teams. His voice takes us there. It illuminates every corner. It gives us the sense that Mets games happen in a world of special, vivid elegance.

Because I love the effect of Gary's perfect voice so much, I wasn't happy when he switched from radio to television at the start of the 2006 season. A lot more people can do television than can do radio. And no one does radio as well as Gary. But this turned out to be one of these Mets decisions I don't initially like that ends up being all right in the end (there aren't a lot of these, but there are some). Tom McCarthy slipped in to replace Gary on the radio. I say slipped in because his voice is so much like Gary's that he can fool you into thinking that he is Gary for extended periods. You feel as if you are trying to distinguish between Coke and Diet Coke. I'm glad the Mets understood the need for this gentle transition. The Mets broadcast teams have been so stable over the years that Mets fans would find it harder than fans of other teams to suddenly find themselves in a baseball universe created by an unfamiliar voice.

Moving Gary to television also made it possible for the new Mets television station, SNY, to win the fans over immediately with the unbelievably good television broadcasting team of Cohen, Darling, and Hernandez. Ron Darling and Keith Hernandez have none of the blandness that jocks often have in the broadcasting booth. Darling has a loose, friendly, informal style, and a voice that sounds a little like Wally Cleaver's on *Leave It to Beaver*. Keith has that querulous voice you hear on the *Seinfeld* episode. Rather than sounding like jocks, Keith and Ron sound like thoughtful fans who somehow managed to get into the bodies of famous Mets, where they learned things that most fans can only imagine. I enjoy their humility and humor, and the fact that they really seem to know what they're talking about. I forgive Keith for sometimes putting his foot in his mouth. But what I enjoy most is Gary in the middle, bringing it all together, keeping everything smooth, oiled, and coherent, with his rich golden tone between the two funny voices of the athletes.

2006: Getting Ahead

As the 2006 season began, Mets fans were hopeful but they were holding themselves back. We hoped that Beltran would calm down and relax and play well enough not to be booed. We weren't sure that he would. Alomar hadn't. We hoped that Delgado, acquired in the off season, would be what he had always been. We hoped that Florida hadn't gotten his last good season. We didn't count on anything. We knew what often happened when older stars came here. They lost something in the lights.

We also remembered that we had been hopeful at the start of every season since 2000. It had become embarrassing and we didn't want to be so pitiful, so desperate, and so ridiculous all over again. When the 2006 season began, and I made my predictions, I picked the Mets to finish third, behind unfathomable Atlanta and the promising Phillies. I looked at the Mets and I thought I saw a first place team. But I wouldn't be caught believing my eyes again.

The season began and the Mets went into first place and they stayed there.

Everything fired. The team settled into a kind of serenity of domination that promised more than 100 victories. And if there hadn't been injuries, we would have had our 100. At the center of the lineup, Beltran, Delgado, and Wright were three balanced, harmonious, and equal offensive forces. When have three men at the heart of a lineup ever driven in 116, 114, and 116 runs? That says it all somehow. If one man slumped, the other pistons could pick up the pace.

There was no Beltran-like drama with Delgado. He didn't have a learning curve. He just came and placed his left-handed bat, and his 38 home runs, right in the middle of this symmetry. Beltran astonished everyone, giving us a better season than anyone expected from him, with roadtrips on which he would simply and quietly win game after game. In the first half of 2006, we learned that Wright and Reyes had not reached cruising altitude at 22. They were 23 and still climbing. How much better could they get? And who were all these guys we never heard of who came to us and played like stars? We thought Paul LoDuca would give us the defensively skilled, offensively challenged catcher most teams lived with. But he became our beloved Paulie, an amazing clutch hitter, a tough, riveting presence, with a .318 batting average! And who was this Xavier Nady, or Jose Valentin, or Endy Chavez? Where had they come from? What were they doing here? Had anyone, even Omar, known that they were going to be this good?

The old pitchers, the old masters, were steady. Glavine and Martinez, the Hall-of-Famers, began their seasons as All-Stars. The middle relievers were amazingly reliable, after a few anomalies were eliminated. And we had a fine closer in Billy Wagner, a little self-proclaimed hillbilly who threw almost 100 mph. The team played like a contented machine. When someone slumped, someone would pick up. Nothing looked like it was even thinking of going wrong.

The Mets of 2006 were like a runner in a dream, going fast but feeling as if he is in slow motion, wondering how he could be so far in front, wondering why no one was gaining on him or keeping up with him. Am I awake or asleep, he asks himself, am I alive or dead? He feels himself to make sure he is whole. He listens but there is nothing but silence. He hopes that when he finally crosses the finish line, his apparent triumph will finally seem real.

It stayed unreal. The Mets were whole. They were alive and awake. Nobody else ever got good. Not Atlanta. Not the Phillies. In 2006, the Mets took off early and that was it. You kept expecting there to be more of a story, but there wasn't. It was over by the All-Star break. You spent the whole summer enjoying them, watching them win, waiting for the postseason to start so that the story could continue.

Pedro Martinez

I like to think that Pedro Martinez was always destined to be a Met. The way he pitches has always reminded me of Tom Seaver. He has power and variety and perfect placement. He has more innings pitched than hits and walks combined. Once he gets past the first inning, and knows what is working, he seems to be in an iron groove. No one can touch him until he tires.

When he came to us in 2005, Pedro pitched an absolutely typical Seaver season. An E.R.A. below 3. More than 200 strikeouts. A 15–8 record that should have been something like 20–6 but wasn't because this was the .500 level Mets. There was the same adaptability as Seaver had, the same rock-steady intelligence. There was the same noble competence and patience.

But if Pedro pitched like Tom Seaver, his personality was more like Tug McGraw's. Pedro is a thoughtful eccentric. A philanthropist and a gardener, a joker in a jacket, you have to love him. When the "Vote for Pedro" shirts started to appear at Shea, I thought it was terrific. Pedro could have come out of the world of *Napoleon Dynamite*. He seems to be entirely sane and just a little bit crazy. Ebullient in the dugout, he is almost grim on the mound. He stares at the catcher with something that looks disconcertingly like sadness and regret. But he is just concentrating. And he knows exactly what he is doing.

Fate washed Pedro up onto other shores, but when he came to us, it seemed as if he was the one destined to lead us out of our early millennial rut. Didn't the coming of Pedro prove that Omar was real? Wasn't it a sign of Omar's grace and power? Now that Omar had brought Pedro to lead us, wouldn't everything be different?

Everything was immediately different. In 2005, we felt, behind Pedro, as if we might soon be champions again. Though the team, in 2005, wasn't worthy of him, he never complained. He was patient and content to inspire others to be worthy of him. In part thanks to Pedro, Carlos Delgado agreed to join us in 2006. Carlos Beltran would eventually become more comfortable. Jose Reyes would grow into a superstar. Maybe these things had nothing to do with Pedro, but he seemed to be involved with them somehow. Pedro changed what we expected of the Mets.

The 2006 season began as well as it possibly could have for Pedro Martinez. Without the 95 mph fastball he once had, he became one of the smartest, most surprising, most unsettling pitchers I have ever seen a batter face. He spent the first half of the 2006 season waving away the opposition, removing all obstacles, clearing a path to the championship. By the time Pedro faltered in midseason, the team knew where it was going and how it would get there. Pedro went on the disabled list for a while, and we waited patiently for him to come back. Let him rest up good, we thought, we don't need him now, but we'll really need him in the postseason.

When Pedro came back, he was mysteriously not any good any more. When it became clear that there was actually something wrong with him, we learned, at first, that he had torn a calf muscle. But then we learned that he needed rotator cuff surgery, and that he would not be coming back to us until late in the 2007 season. Who really knew what he would be able to do then, after shoulder surgery in his late thirties?

I don't want Pedro Martinez to remain what he is now: a transitional figure separating two Mets eras. I want him to be a great Met. I want him to be part of our eternal rotation, with Seaver, Koosman, Matlack, Gooden, Darling, Fernandez, Ojeda, Cone, and Leiter. I want to see him win a game for us in the World Series. I want to see him coming down off the mound, pointing to the sky and giving thanks. I want him to enter the Promised Land with the rest of us.

Carlos Beltran

Carlos Beltran has very round, bovine eyes and a little boy's full lips. He looks as if he could be hurt very easily. And I spent all of 2005 wondering if the stupid fans booing him were hurting him. I think they were. I think that those Shea fans who boo should take some responsibility for the fact that Carlos had, in 2005, a completely generic year. If he had had a season, okay, not as great as 2006, but halfway between 2005 and 2006, we would have won the Wild Card. I wish I could boo the fans who booed him.

"You gotta be tough to play in this town." If I hear that one more time, I'll strangle the person who says it. It is tough enough to play in this town, with the endless, invasive media swarm. Fans who like to boo shouldn't make it worse. And I am not just appealing to their senses of justice and decency. I am talking numbers in the win column. You want that? You shut your stupid booing mouth.

I was at the second game played at Shea in 2006. When Carlos came up, I heard some boos. Sure I mostly heard cheers, but can you believe that there are fans stupid enough to boo a superstar coming off a mediocre season, trying to make a comeback, on the second home game of the season? It's enough to make you ashamed to be a human being.

Anyway, Carlos blew everybody away in 2006. Everybody, even the booers. I'll admit that I didn't think he could do it. I'll admit that I thought the Mets were overrating him when they signed him to that big contract. I figured decent average, some speed, some power, excellent defense, but not really a superstar. As we went into the 2006 season, I felt that I would be overjoyed if Carlos Beltran managed to hit 25 home runs and drive in 100 runs.

But guess what? Carlos is a superstar. I was wrong. Most of us were wrong. That 38 homer season wasn't a fluke. Omar was right when he said that this guy was one of the best players in the game. Look at what he did. Watching him in 2006 was like watching Seaver, Piazza, or Gooden in their prime. A slugging percentage of .600? Ted Williams. Hall of Fame. Look at that swing! Look at how many home runs Carlos hit without ever looking as if he is trying to hit a home run. Look at the liquid, loping grace with which he caught what seemed like three-quarters of the balls hit into the entire outfield.

Carlos is great and he's young and we have him. And he's not one of these superstars who come here when the toothpaste tube is almost squeezed out and there are just one or two more brushfuls in it. Carlos could have ten years like this in him. And what would happen if he could reach the point where he is as comfortable hitting at Shea as he is on the road? Forget about it.

But Carlos really has to learn not to be afraid. He's so quiet and shy. You won't see him on Letterman. He's happy to play like a centerpiece, but he doesn't want to be a centerpiece. That is okay. There are enough centerpieces on the Mets. Let's take Beltran as he is. And I will hope and pray that if 2006 was a career year, he won't be held responsible for not reaching these heights in coming years.

Already I'm anxious. Carlos had a perfect season and I have to be anxious! What if he hits only 25 home runs next year, and drives in only 100 runs?

Wouldn't you know it? Carlos hits 41 home runs, drives in 116 runs, scores 127 (wow!), but there he is at the plate with the bat on his shoulder at the precise moment the 2006 season ends. That was quite a pitch, if you remember. Nobody could have known enough to swing at it. But booers, the hyenas, don't listen to any excuses. They don't see, hear, or think. The evil larynx is ready, like a sphincter that is only happy when it's open.

David Wright

At the plate, David Wright looks like a squirrel, crossed with Orlando Bloom perhaps, but still a squirrel. He squints and sticks out his tongue. He blows out his breath and shows his upper teeth. After he swings, he sticks the bat under his left shoulder, fiddles with his batting gloves, and then wipes his face with the top of his jersey.

He is always moving. He doesn't daydream and he doesn't space out. Everything gets a glance from his eyes or a twitch from his mouth. Like a kid in an arcade, he is totally interactive. It makes me nervous to look at him, but David is the man I'd want at the plate if the Mets were down to their final out. Somebody who is always in motion is not a fatalist.

Defensively, David's still not a complete player. Sometimes he plays third like Brooks Robinson and sometimes he looks as if he doesn't know what the round thing is coming towards him. But at the plate the fidgeting kid doesn't hit like a fidgeting kid. He hits like a master, like Williams or Musial. The fidgeting must be his way of honing in on things. I don't know. All I know is what I have seen him do, and what I expect him to do when he comes to the plate. David hits for high average. And he has lots of power. He is incredible in the clutch. In 2006, he had 20 home runs and 74 RBIs by the All-Star Break. He hits like he could be the MVP next year, or the year after, or any year of the next twenty. The Mets have never had an MVP. Not in 45 years. David is good enough and strong enough to win a Triple Crown. No one on any team has done that for almost 40 years.

The day after he hit a home run in his first All-Star game, David was a guest on David Letterman's show. I worried about this. Athletes don't always field Letterman's irony very well. But David was all right. He came out in real clothes and you could see for the first time how truly big his hands and shoulders are. His head and shoulders moved from side to side as he answered every question, sometimes even before it was out of Letterman's mouth.

He was scrubbed down to his skin. He smiled a lot and made sweet little awkward jokes, about how he always kissed up to teachers, about his brothers making fun of his fielding, about needing the tongue that he sticks out so much. He was nice about everybody, and he seemed so pleased to be so admired and so young. He was totally charming, because he was who he was. Although he was never still, I don't think he was nervous. He realizes that the world will come around to him. Because he is a wonder.

Great young players are usually personally rough in some way. There's something excitingly unattractive about them, before they get rubbed smooth and polished. David's not like this. He is beautiful and he is complete. He has this "winning" smile. He's looks like what they used to call a "matinee idol." There's something retro about him. I'll bet he doesn't have a tattoo.

In the second half of the season, David slowed down a little. He may have tired himself out with his gargantuan effort in the home run derby before the All-Star game. He only hit a few more home runs for the season, ending up with 26. But his average stayed up above .300, and the doubles kept coming, and he finished the season with 116 RBIs. When the Mets clinched the Division title, David was the center of the celebration, the life of the party, the handsome, smiling soul of this happy loving team. He looked like he had just been born, full-formed. He was so fresh-faced and dripping and wide-eyed and wet in the locker room and on the field as he reached into the stands to slap the fans' hands, still holding his bottle of champagne, with a stogie stuck in his smiling mouth.

I'll be an old man when this kid retires. After a few more years, his mastery won't seem miraculous. It will have become familiar. That's a loss. But it won't go away for a very long time. Instead of the dreaming his talent now gives me, I'll have all these games and moments and pennants and championships to remember. This is the natural sequence of things, if things go as well as they possibly can. This is what we had with Seaver, until they traded him away. This is what we should have had with Gooden and Strawberry. We didn't really have it with Piazza, or Hernandez or Carter, because they were not with us at the beginning.

Come to think of it, we've never really had it, have we? We've never really seen the beginning, the middle, and the end of the career of a Hall-of-Famer. Oh, please let David be a Met at forty. I would love to enjoy remembering what I see of him now. I would love to recognize the kid in the veteran, jittery at the plate, and running the bases as he always has, with his back up straight and his arms paddling at his side.

David reminds me of Seaver and Koosman when they came up. They were as young, but like him, they didn't seem half-finished. Like him, they were already as good as the best of the older guys. They were like the Beatles who, in 1964, left a strange mark on Shea stadium that, in the minds of those who fill its stands, never went away. The Beatles were very young, and very good-looking. And they were so much better than any of the older people who tried in vain to find the imperfections of immaturity in the wonderful things they did.

Like the Beatles, and like Seaver and Koosman, David Wright shows you that youth is not just passion and energy, without order or control. Sometimes a beautiful young person snags a piece of the sun and just rides it.

Jose Reyes

Jose Reyes always looks like he thinks he's getting away with something. He has a grin and a strange little beard that make him look like a satyr. And what's with the eyes? Are those human eyes? They look like the eyes of a cartoon fox.

Jose is just like a fox in a cartoon. With charm and good humor, he robs everybody blind. Everything he does feels like some kind of trick. He's like a magician and he's like a crook. You've watched enough baseball. You think you know what's possible and what isn't? You don't.

Fast little shortstops are a pain, but at least they're not a power threat. Right? Balls that bounce in the outfield and are fielded right away by outfielders are singles. Right? Leadoff hitters don't drive in very many runs. Right? You certainly couldn't add together their runs scored and runs batted in and get a number larger than 200, could you? That would be incredible. That would be sublime. Think of it. He can actually do this. Jose is so perfectly unique that he encourages you to go nuts imagining all kinds of number patterns you never dreamed you'd see. In 2006, he came very close to becoming the first 20–20–20–20 man (homers, doubles, triples, stolen bases). He did become the second 80–60 man ever (RBIs, stolen bases). I think he might be able to be the first to have a slugging percentage over .500, a batting average over .300, and then whatever number of stolen bases Willie Mays never had. Jose has a shot at becoming the first 20–120–100–20–20–60 man (home runs, runs, RBIs, doubles, triples, stolen bases) and if he is, he will be the last until they perfect genetic engineering.

Jose doesn't believe that the laws of Newtonian physics apply to him in the way that they apply to everyone else. When he steals a base or takes an extra one, he loves to dive head first. You want to scream when he does that. How can it possibly be faster to do that? You have to break your momentum. You have to slow down to get into the dive, don't you? But there is something about diving head first that is a perfect image for what this man does. His head comes towards you, his crazy curls flying, and then suddenly you don't see his head anymore. Where did it go? He's like an electron in quantum mechanics. Where is he? He's down around your ankles. Now he's back in your face. He dived and bounced up and clapped his hands all in a single motion. He's Gumby! How the hell can somebody do that?

When Jose comes to the plate, I feel like a fountain of adrenalin. I sing the silly Jose song, which is lame in the way that only a true and heartfelt love song can be. JO-SAYYYYYY! JO-SAY! JO-SAY! JO-SAY! JO-SAYYY! JO-SAYYY!, JO-SAYYYYYY! JO-SAY! JO-SAY! JO-SAY! JO-SAYYY! JO-SAYYY! There's something unnerving about this absurdist chant, and I think that the Cardinals found it unnerving in the NLCS. They just didn't find it unnerving enough. They mocked it in the clubhouse at Shea after their seventh game victory. That's the problem with chants. They can be turned against you very easily. Still, the Jose chant is great and it will last. We'll use it again. And next time our team will sing it in the clubhouse in the spray of champagne.

Has there ever been a ballplayer as exciting as Jose Reyes? Has there ever been a left side of the infield so young and so talented? Has there ever been more of a reason for Mets fans to feel so good about the next fifteen years? Well, maybe. Let's not think about it.

Paul LoDuca

Where the hell did Paulie LoDuca come from? I would be lying if I said that I had ever been conscious of his existence before he came to the Mets. I kind of knew that the Dodgers had a catcher with that name but I had never really paid attention. I was shocked to look him up and see that he was 34 and had been playing regularly for years. In the Piazza era, we had a sense that we had Piazza and everybody else just had the generic eighth-place hitting catcher. Don't get me wrong. We had respect for these guys because they could do things like throw out baserunners trying to steal second. But they were all the same guy, except for our guy who was the greatest catcher ever, even though he couldn't do a few things the generic catchers could do.

So LoDuca comes to us and leads a team like ours in batting average? What's going on? I know it must be something of an advantage to hit after Jose Reyes and before a murderer's row of Beltran, Delgado, and Wright. I might be able to manage .250 hitting in that spot. But LoDuca takes some amazing advantage of his golden slot. He stands there with the bat, looking so thick and tough and so anxious to make a difference in the game. And how many times have you been rewarded with that harsh and quick line drive bouncing in for a single or going all the way to the wall? Oh Paulie you are beautiful, you say as Jose races around the bases and you think of the guys who will now be able to come up.

The Mets tried to make it seem as if Paulie was a kid from Brooklyn. Well he was born in Brooklyn, but he grew up in Arizona. Still, when they played "Staying Alive" as he came to the plate, we were invited to think of him striding down an avenue in Bay Ridge with a can of paint in his hand. We didn't buy it. They had tried to do the same thing with Mazilli and that left a little bit of a sour taste in our mouths. Truth be told, Paulie is very far from the Travolta type. He's not a Tony Manero, he's a Paulie. He looks more like a thicker version of Pee Wee Herman with really dark eyebrows. But that's cool. Paulie made his own unique impression on this team. He was the hardest and happiest hugger at the clinching. And he was just one of the many unanticipated novelties that made the 2006 season such a deep and lasting pleasure for every Mets fan.

Carlos Delgado

Carlos Delgado has a way of looking like he is the center of the universe. He doesn't look as if he wants to be the center of the universe. He doesn't look as if he thinks he is the center of the universe. He looks as if he IS the center of the universe. To say that the man has presence is a ridiculous understatement.

He has this straight, broad front of a forehead, and this massive and powerful body. But he moves with such ease, and his gaze is so steady. He seems so perfectly relaxed as he makes the rounds of the dugout, laughing and smiling. It calms me down to look at him.

He is better than yoga. He calms his teammates with his unsweating cool. And he calms me with his home runs. He is like Clendenon, Strawberry, and Piazza in that his home runs are always breathtakingly beautiful. He has that terrifyingly authoritative shot that sends the ball way high up into the lights down the right field line. And he has that swift strong slap, with a little bit of a reach out over the plate, that sends the ball, against all logic, out to the scoreboard in center.

Carlos was the anchor of the 2006 team, the one player best-equipped to lead. Wright and Reyes were too young, Beltran was too shy, the pitchers were hurt too much and they were pitchers anyway. Delgado should have been too new, but he wasn't. He was like Donn Clendenon or Keith Hernandez, at home and in front as soon as he arrived. It was his team right away. And he was ours.

2006:
Late Summer Blues

You would think that it's a good thing to get in front in April and then have nobody come close to catching you. It is, but it isn't entirely. The Mets had done something like this in 1986 and we all saw how much fun that was. 2006 was the 20th anniversary of that greatest of all Mets seasons and so it was in the back of our minds all summer. There was even a commemorative reunion, where the great '86 team, older and thicker, showed up to offer the '06 team some of their plentiful excess karma. But this didn't help matters. As good as it was, we knew that the '06 team was not the '86 team. This team was fine, but we knew it wasn't perfect. And we had all of July and August and September to worry about how it wasn't perfect and how it might be vulnerable in October.

The 1986 Mets had one of the best starting pitching staffs in baseball history. In the second half of the 2006 season, it wasn't clear whether or not the Mets even had a starting rotation. El Duque got into an impressive groove, but Pedro Martinez fell away. Glavine had gotten off to one of his great first halves but he too faded before developing some kind of scary nerve problem. Trachsel was reliable in his slow, methodical way, pitching his six innings, giving up his four runs, which was normally enough to keep this particular team in the ballgame. Trachsel would finish up the season with a 1986-Mets record and a 1962-Mets E.R.A. A series of rookies took up the slack and each looked good and each raised questions.

So the pitching was questionable, but the middle relief was so good and the hitting was so good that we continued to win. And we kept on winning even after one of our best middle relievers, Duaner Sanchez, got into a freak taxicab accident that took him out for the rest of the season. If you believed in omens, and all baseball fans do at some level, you could allow yourself to become frightened by several of the things that happened to the Mets in the second half of the 2006 season.

The offense continued to be fabulous, but Wright had mysteriously stopped hitting home runs and there was always one slugger in a slump at any given moment. Sometimes it looked as if it was very easy to shut our fabulous offense down. We lost a number of games to pitchers just because they were left-handed. We lost games to rookies just up from the minors. We won most of our games, but we saw that it wasn't impossible to beat us. Many Mets fans worried that this was a team that was more likely to impress over 162 games than over five or seven. We didn't want to go down to an inferior team in the playoffs. Especially if the Yankees, once again, made it to the World Series.

A lot of New Yorkers, the kind that can root for either team, were tired of the Yankees. Editors at newspapers and magazines kept assigning reporters to write stories about how much more fun and interesting the 2006 Mets were than the 2006 Yankees. All these people who looked like the people on *Sex and the City* were ready to jump on our bandwagon. But those of us who knew the Mets and had lived with the Mets, who looked more like the people on *Seinfeld*, were now really nervous. If all the hype said that the Mets were now going to be New York's favorite team, it was time to tuck the shirt in and pat down the hair and make sure the fly wasn't unzipped. Let alone put on moisturizer, wherever the hell that is supposed to go. We weren't sure that the Mets were ready for their photo-op.

2006: The Clinching

Oh but they were. It all came together at the clinching. The Mets were supposed to clinch the 2006 National League Eastern Division title in Pittsburgh. But the second-place Phillies kept winning. And the Pirates, the last place team in the National League Central, swept us in three games. The Mets had to go back to Shea carrying crates of unopened champagne.

What if the Mets had clinched just because Philadelphia had lost? What if the Mets had clinched when they were off by themselves, where the Allegheny and the Monangahela join to form the Ohio river? That wouldn't have cut it in this particular year. In the end it was lucky that the Mets were forced to clinch in Flushing, where they could feel what they had accomplished in the earthquake of our stadium, where they could bathe not only in champagne, but in the sound that rises up to our lights as screaming fans stand and yell and clap and won't sit down. Mets fans are always the loudest fans, but they were even louder than usual on the night of the clinching because they had waited for all of a spacey summer for just such a moment of triumph. The clinching meant nothing. It was long foreseen and embarrassingly delayed. But it became the high point of our season. We saw what we had. And the Mets heard it.

Have you ever seen a more attractive and sympathetic team than the one that clinched the National League Eastern Division Title at Shea stadium on September 18, 2006? I haven't. Look at them leaping just as they hug. Look at them holding on to each other and jumping up and down. See the spray and the dripping and see them wiping the stinging wet from their eyes. Like contest winners, they tell the reporters that what they are feeling can't be put into words. They all say the same things, but they all talk differently. And they all say that they are all such good friends, that there are no divisions, that there is just brotherhood and a big chain of love that connects them all and connects them with the fans.

Look at them. I love them. There is shy Carlos and big, calm, smiling Carlos. There is tall, gawky Shawn and stiff, uncertain Aaron with his interesting face. There is Lastings the kid who acts like he belongs here. There is Paul LoDuca hooking his arm around Carlos Delgado's head and whispering something in his ear and Carlos looking like he's tearing up. There is the dignity and reserve of Tom Glavine and Steve Trachsel, who pitched the six scoreless innings to win this game. There are David and Jose running out onto the field, hugging and squinting and spraying and slapping the hands of the fans who've remained. David looks like a teenager who has broken into his dad's liquor cabinet and is smoking his finest cigar. Do I know these people? No. Do I want to get to know them more than I do? No, not really. I don't want to know anything about them that might make it harder for me to love them as much as I do as I watch them right now jumping up and down on the screen. I want to see what I see and love what I love. Here are the Mets. I love the Mets. I always love the Mets. And right at this very moment, these guys are the Mets. Individually, they won't always be the Mets but they are the Mets right now. They are so diverse, and so giddy and happy to be all together as a team, that you feel as if you are looking at some kind of idyll of what New York and America can be. You get sentimental and simplistic perhaps, but your happiness is as real as theirs and your pleasure in the sense of a community is just as strong. It's exactly as the players are saying. It's unbelievable. It's amazing. It's such a great group of guys. It's such a great group of fans. What you're feeling can't be put into words that make much more sense than this.

In the end, all the embarrassment of the delay is forgotten. The clinching at Shea is a revelation of the team that will take us into the playoffs for the first time in six years, to win us a flag we haven't waved in twenty!

Doris from Rego Park

When the Mets clinched the pennant on September 18, 2006, thousands of Mets fans gathered on the mets.com fan forum message board as if it were Times Square. Thrilled and sentimental, they posted heartfelt words on a pile of threads. Overcome with his emotion, someone proposed that we think of the Mets as having won the division title this year for Bob Murphy, the beloved announcer for the team from 1962 to 2004, who had recently died of cancer. There was much enthusiasm for this dedication, as if it were ours to make. And then someone proposed that we also dedicate it to Doris of Rego Park, who had died a few years ago. Waterworks all around. For Murph and for Doris. They were to stand for all the dead Mets fans. Tug was soon added. And Danny Frisella, a minor relief pitcher for the team who had died thirty years ago in a dune buggy accident. We soon had our pantheon, to which each of us privately made several personal additions.

Who was Doris of Rego Park and why did she mean so much to so many Mets fans? If you listened to talk radio during the baseball season in New York in the nineties, you knew that Doris was a sweet and slightly spacey woman with a chronic cough who knew and remembered everything about the Mets and had dedicated her life to them. She'd call in and offer her sense of what was happening with the team and the talk show hosts treated her softly and kindly as if she was a beloved aunt. There was always room for Doris of Rego Park and you were always happy to hear her voice. She became the most famous Mets fan who was famous simply for being a Mets Fan. She was like the Cow-Bell Man of the radio talk shows.

In the world in which we are bodies and not just voices or words, Doris was Doris Bauer, a child of Holocaust refugees who suffered from Elephant Man's Disease and from autistic compulsions. She lived with her mother in Rego Park. She worked as an administrator, and she died at the age of 58 from cancer. Her physical impairments and her compulsions made her the perfect Mets fan. You could tell from her calls that nothing could interfere with the intensity with which she had focused her spirit on the Mets. We were all awed and envious, in the way, I imagine, that religious people think of saints who have devoted every waking moment of their lives to spiritual discipline.

Doris had her Sunday season ticket, the ham sandwiches and shrimp cocktails she lived on, her job and her mother and her brother's family, and the radio talk shows. She made a life that can't help but fascinate us. I saw a Broadway play recently (*The Drowsy Chaperone*) about a man who sits in his chair in his sweater in his apartment and just listens to and dreams about the world of Broadway. Doris did something like this. There are certain things that can give you a life even if circumstances get in the way of you having the kind of life that other people have. If you work hard enough, these things become not a substitute for life but more like a legitimate alternative. Broadway can be like this. And so can baseball. It is satisfying and mysterious. If you engage it in the right way, it is never boring in the way that most people's lives are boring. It gives you friends and models and mentors and cautionary stories. It gives you a community. It gives you a life.

I think this is a good thing. I know it isn't always. I am pleased that my widowed mother, who can hardly walk now, has the Mets during the season. But I know how bereft she is when the season ends. For Doris baseball was good. For my mother it is both good and bad. For me it is a diversion. But sometimes I think about how if something really horrible happened to me, it might have to become my life.

2006: The Hour of the Wolf

After the Mets clinched, some not very good things happened. I remember hearing once that there's this ancient Scandinavian belief that the hour before the dawn is the hour of the wolf, the hour when ghosts and demons are most active, the hour in which the sleepless encounter their deepest fears.

Well, we had an hour of the wolf. At first it didn't seem very serious. The Mets lost a few games after the clinching and it was easy enough to say that they were just relaxing a little before the pressure of the postseason. But it was more than that. Some of the fears we had during the season were taking on a kind of demonic life. We lost Pedro Martinez. It felt as if we lost him twice, once to the torn calf muscle, and once to the torn rotator cuff. We turned to Orlando Hernandez, El Duque, the great postseason pitcher who had had such a great second half with us, and who would now be our ace. Then, practicing for his opening game start against the Dodgers, El Duque tore a calf muscle. A calf muscle? Him a calf muscle too? Tore a calf muscle in practice? What a fluke. Had that ever happened before?

We were left with Glavine and Trachsel as our aces. But what was happening in the life of Steve Trachsel? Why did he miss his all-important last start, his final practice start, so important to his rhythm, to go home to attend to a family problem whose nature was never specified? When had a player ever done anything like this before? Could we rely on Trachsel? We had dominated the National League all year. How was it possible that we were going into the postseason with a starting pitching staff of just Glavine and Maine?

It was a scary moment for Mets fans. There was that awful feeling that if we lost, we would have an excuse. And that is not what you want to be thinking when you go into the postseason.

But then we swept the Dodgers in three games. And in the last game, we came back from a four-run deficit in Los Angeles. I felt like I was at that point in a novel in which a character you've been expecting to die has miraculously managed to survive. Everything was going to be all right, I thought. This was a team of destiny. Despite having suffered what looked like a fatal blow, the Mets made it clear that nothing could prevent them from demolishing whatever token opposition the National League offered them. If we could handle the Dodgers easily, we would certainly handle the Cardinals, who weren't even as good as the Dodgers. We might lose in the end to the Tigers or the A's. We might have lost to the Yankees. But we were certainly not going to lose to the Cardinals.

And so we had our triumphant moment, our moment of resurrection. We had survived the first round of the playoffs. The Yankees hadn't. We were ready for our real close-up this time, our biggest moment in six years, on our way to our biggest moment in twenty. But then Cory Lidle, a journeyman pitcher who had been with the Yankees for four months, on a joy ride up the East River, crashed his plane into an apartment house on the Upper East Side. And so the airwaves and press were filled with details of the crash and heartfelt tributes to someone who had never really spent much time in the sports headlines before. You couldn't complain. Cory Lidle was a real person who had suffered a real tragedy. The playoffs were just a game. So you had to wait quietly and without complaint as our great moment was ruined. How weird was this championship season going to get?

Going to a Playoff Game: 2006 NLDS Game Two

I went to the second NLDS playoff game against the Dodgers, the one in which Tom Glavine pitched so beautifully. I had won the lottery. At 12 noon on the appointed day, I had opened both of the browsers on my computer, and a timer gave each of the browsers a shot at getting through every sixty seconds. For 45 minutes, I switched from one browser to the other. Finally one browser got through and I bought my tickets.

My daughter and I got to the game two and a half hours early. There was still room to park in the parking lot, which had become a big café of folding chairs and tables, and bundled up people burning things on grates. The atmosphere was hysterically festive. Mets fans were daring to be brave and hopeful because we had won the first game. Sonia and I went into the stadium, but they wouldn't let us see batting practice from the field boxes, the way they normally do. So we went to the loge and took pictures. There was nothing to take pictures of yet. There was the mindless, everyday, ordinary zen of batting practice. People were standing around and chatting in the outfield as outfielders caught balls between them. You saw the press and players and unidentifiable VIPs. We looked at the crowd on the field through the binoculars my father had bought in Tokyo in 1951, when he was fighting in Korea. The binoculars looked as if they had been made yesterday but their leather case was worn and old and beautiful. We had brought these binoculars to our first game at Shea, in 1964. My father showed me how to focus them. Through them, I saw Sandy Koufax clearly. I saw Casey Stengel, his head on his hand, sound asleep in the Mets dugout.

This time we managed to see Ron Darling in a yellow suit and John Franco in a grey one and Gary Cohen in a blue shirt, standing around and talking. Nothing at all was happening. You smelled people's hot dogs. You saw the sunset and the full moon. And you thought of what the place would look like in two hours.

We got our hot dogs and knishes and diet Pepsi, and sought out the long escalators that take you all the way to the top. At the top we looked out at the ruins of the Worlds Fair, and the soft, boxy sprawl of Queens, darkening into a carpet of diamonds. Everything looked and felt beautiful. We were at a playoff game and we could not believe our luck. And it was luck that we were there, nothing but. I had won a lottery. My e-mail address had been picked. I was with 56,000 people at something that a million people would have given anything to attend.

We found our seats and gasped with happiness when we saw our view. Oh, you could hardly see the players, and if the Dodgers had played in the Mets uniforms and the Mets had played in the Dodgers' uniforms, we would not have been able to tell that the teams had been switched. But we saw everything: the whole stadium, the whole Whitestone Bridge, the Whitestone Expressway, the Van Wyck, and all of Flushing, the beginnings of Long Island Sound. We were on top of it all, right by the tall and orange and famous foul pole.

The stadium was filling up. My two sisters arrived and we were all together, way up so high. Ralph Kiner threw out the first ball, ambling to and from the mound in a bright yellow sweater. The anthem was sung. The uniforms of the Mets, as they took the field, seemed whiter than they had ever been.

By the middle of the second inning, the stadium was full. Each level of the stands was filled with thickly clothed people, illuminated in silvery iridescence, or dim in dark valleys of shadow, in which you could see flashbulbs flickering every second like fireflies.

The crowd was ridiculously loud and active, as if it was clear to everyone that as Mets fans we were supposed to be louder and crazier than all other fans. Every pitch was an event. People stood up whenever there were two strikes on a Dodger or three balls on a Met, which made no sense at all but was fun.

It was not a game of big events and great moments. It was a game of smooth superior play, by a team enjoying the comforting, rising, receding swells of our sound. It was a game of singles and runs, of fine starting pitching and fine relief. When it was over, the happy Mets were up two game to none. We were happy too, as we came down from our seats in the heavens, slapping strangers' hands, glad to have so many ramps to the ground.

Cardinal Red

Game 1 of the NLCS was exactly what it was supposed to be. Tom Glavine stepped up with another paternal pitching performance, something that gave us reason to continue to believe that the collapse of our pitching rotation was not a cause for worry. Carlos Beltran hit a home run, and Endy Chavez and Jose Valentin's each saved the game with the kind of defensive plays you only seem to see in the postseason. This was the Mets' eighth win in a row. It had begun to seem as if they would never lose again. Oh, sure they would. We didn't expect to beat Carpenter in the second game. We might, of course, but we weren't expecting it.

Well, we did get to Carpenter. And Carlos Delgado hit two home runs. A high shot to right, a slap to center. 450 feet just with the power of his arms. Jose Reyes was back in his groove, running around the bases with his flying curls. What a team we had! Already, by the sixth inning, we were thinking ahead in happy, practical ways, about the challenge of Detroit's fine young pitchers.

Then all of a sudden we lost. We lost the lead, and then we regained it and then we lost it a second, final time. Mota and Wagner, who had been as reliable down the stretch as any relievers could be, collapsed. Both of them.

This could not possibly be significant. This would be forgotten, wouldn't it? Such a fluky game would not live forever in our memories, would it? No. On Saturday in St. Louis Steve Trachsel would steady us. Older guys were good at this. Dad would come out again, to where we were by the side of the highway. He'd change the tire and we'd all drive home.

I'm still not sure what happened. Suddenly Trachsel, a man we had learned to sort of rely on (always sort of, always rely) was headed for oblivion. After one of the ugliest opening innings in Mets history, this clearly troubled and distracted man was transformed into a shade cleaning out his locker. For the first time in the long and glorious season, we were behind somebody else. Down two games to one. All of the "Ya Gotta Believe" stuff, all the old Mets-as-underdog stuff was taken out of the hall closet, dusted off and hung from the railings. The Mets were acting like the Mets. It was like '86. It would be like '86. When had the Mets ever avoided making things as exciting as things could be made?

The fourth game was good. It restored some perspective. There's something about playoff baseball that makes you think that the last thing that happened is all that there is. When of course it's not. To be honest, ever since the collapse of Mota and Wagner, followed by the collapse of Trachsel, I hadn't really believed. I was afraid I was back in something like 1988, after Scioscia's home run. But then in the fourth game, I saw the Mets again for what they really were this year. I had watched them all season. What could have ever made me doubt that they could play a game like game four, that they could score 12 runs and win commandingly, beautifully.

This was a relief. I was calmer. Even if we lost the fifth game, we should be able to take two at Shea. In spite of the reassuring win in game 4, I was thoroughly sick and tired of the St. Louis Cardinals. They were beginning to freak me out. Is it my imagination or were the 2006 Cardinals a very funny-looking team? Several of them looked like angry babies, several of them had hair that fell unpleasantly onto the back of their beefy necks. And then there was that blood-purple flap of hair on Spiezio's chin.

Whatever the Cardinals were trying to do, by looking like this, was working. On me, at least. The Cardinals seemed a lot more menacing than their 83 wins entitled them to be. And there was something about the sea of red around them, and the hankies flapping like the hair on Spiezio's chin or Belliard's nape, that made me afraid and a little grossed out. Then came that six-run inning in the fourth game, which changed everything, and restored my conviction that the Mets would win the pennant. If the Cardinals wanted to win the pennant, let them do it in one of those years when they were really good. They have enough of them. This was our year. And this was the Tigers' year. This was the Series we all deserved, between two amazing, surprising teams, the best in their leagues.

Then the Cardinals managed to get to Glavine. He had enough rest. He had pitched two wonderful games in a row. But he couldn't hold them this time. After winning Game Five, this crappy, runty, ugly team that had only won 83 games in the regular season was one win away from a pennant. So we all went back to Shea. We would win the next two. At Shea.

Another Playoff Game: 2006 NLCS Game Six

I was at Game Six of the NLCS against the Cardinals. I waited for the people I was meeting by Gate A, behind the little outdoor studio set up for Gary Cohen and Ron Darling. Gary and Ron were immaculate in their suits and ties, sitting in director's chairs on a raised platform under bright lights that lit up the plane trees. They looked as if they were having dinner in a fancy outdoor restaurant in France or LA.

Except that thousands of people were walking by them, dressed in all of the colors of the rainbow except red, yellow, green, indigo, or violet. There were people in jerseys from Seaver to Green, people with orange wigs, and one guy who looked like an accountant dressed in an American flag outfit with a blue and orange face. A big crowd gathered behind the two men in suits, making noise continuously, aware that it was their responsibility to show how psyched the crowd would be tonight. There was a sense that the Mets were home. We knew what we had to do.

We would be, as we have been before, the tenth man on the field. No other fans had our lung power, no other fans were so free of the restraint that keeps most people from painting themselves, singing in public, or booing a called ball. We were the raucous soul of the mighty city you saw from the escalators as you climbed to the upper deck. Okay, I live in Connecticut and the people I was meeting live in Montclair. But we are part of this. Our folks played stickball on Brooklyn streets and snuck into Ebbets field. We can still scream as loud as anybody.

As I was waiting, I saw a little boy about nine years old in the crowd behind Gary and Ron. He was on his father's shoulders, and he was holding and pumping a sign that said "Ya Gotta Believe/Remember '86." The kid couldn't have been born before 1997. Yet he knew Tug's mantra from '73. He knew that '86 meant something. Okay, maybe he didn't. Maybe these were just the feelings of the graying, sweating fortyish guy whose face I couldn't see behind his son's legs. But the kid was pumping that sign, as if what he held in his hand was the key to the Mets' victory tonight.

You can't kill something like this. You can't bury a spirit like this under any number of years of disappointment. Millions of people love to be Mets fans. They love it so that they can have a moment like this. They just want to get together with all these friends and family and scream and jump and shout. We were all anticipating how happy we would be if we won the next two games.

As the stadium filled, as game time approached, the Diamond Vision showed Judy Garland in the *Wizard of Oz*, with her ruby red slippers, closing her eyes and chanting: "There's no place like home." Everybody knew this. Everybody responded. They should have also put up the scene from *Peter Pan* where you clap your hands as loud as you can so that Tinkerbell doesn't die.

Tinkerbell didn't die. And the evening showed how true it was that there is no place like home. Throughout the evening, through the binoculars, I saw how happy the Mets were in the great bath of crowd noise. At points we may have given them a jolt, but I think it was more that we provided a big featherbed on which they could relax, after having been in a witch's castle where snotty hankies had been waved at them by scary red monkeys with chin hair.

It was so much fun. We saw how loud we could be when Jose Reyes hit his leadoff home run and we could do the Jose song at top volume right away. Most people in their whole lives will never hear what rookie John Maine heard as he walked back to the dugout. And when Paul LoDuca hit his two-run single, we felt what Hemingway suggested you only feel maybe once in a lifetime. The stadium moved. I'm not trying to be poetic here. I don't mean that I was so overcome with emotion that it seemed as if the ground was shaking. No. The fricking thing moved. Literally. The concrete bounced and twanged like a guitar string. It was scary. It was wonderful.

The ninth inning was scary too. Not wonderful. We gave Billy Wagner the welcome he deserved because of the incredible season he gave us. But Wagner didn't pitch as well as he should have. He gave up two runs and I began to feel a hellish foreboding when I realized that Albert Pujols could end up taking a big dump on our wonderful season. But the third out came. And it was good. And as strangers slapped hands and sang the Jose song and chanted "Lets Go Mets" and loudly and politely emptied the stadium, we all felt that we had done well and that the Mets were beautiful and that tomorrow night they would win the pennant they had earned.

The End of the 2006 Season

I wish I had been at the seventh game of the NLCS, because I've heard that the consoling solidarity of the crowd, on the ramps and in the train cars, was beautiful. There was the gentleness and kindness of the big crowd that surprised the world on 9/11, but didn't surprise New Yorkers. Alone in my suburban living room with my weeping daughter, I missed the crowd.

The 2006 season was six and a half happy months of greatness. Our team was dominant and glorious. In spite of the sudden disappearance of our starting pitching at the very end, we swept the Dodgers in the first round of the playoffs. We took the Cardinals to the last strike of the ninth inning of the seventh game of the NLCS. We deserved to go further.

In that last game, Endy Chavez brought a ball back to the field after it had cleared the fence. Oliver Perez came back to life. Things felt right. There are many ways the game could have been won by the Mets. I don't have to list them. Nobody screwed up. The big loud crowd did all it could. In the top of the ninth, Yadier Molina hit a ball too high for Endy to catch. In the bottom of the ninth, the Mets filled the bases. The beautiful season struggled to live until the very last second, when you saw the ball drop into the strike zone, you saw the umpire's arm, you saw men jumping, and you scrambled to find the remote. This is baseball. Over the long term, it pleases you. But when the story stops, and the TV is suddenly silent, you really hear that silence.

I am thinking of what continues, and what persists. I imagine the kindness of the defeated crowd. Obviously some people were angry and bitter. But that can't last. If the fruit of disappointment can only be anger and bitterness, the fans of the New York Mets would be one sick and scary bunch of people by now. They would not know how to console each other on the trains back to Manhattan or Manhasset.

Chris Russo, when it was over, said he was upset with the Mets for not being more upset with their loss. Chris would say this. He lives in a kind of failure-free zone. He could be wrong about everything, he could know nothing about nothing, he could be the world's biggest jerk, but as long as people continue to listen to him, he hasn't failed. Carlos Beltran and David Wright live in a more complex world. So do the rest of us. You can be great and gutsy and not a jerk and still take a called third strike, when someone has thrown you a terrific curve ball that looks high as it's coming in. All of us do stuff like this all the time.

Sure I thought Willie Randolph should have sent Chris Woodward up to bunt the runners over instead of sending up Cliff. On the face of it, putting Cliff up looked like a dumb move, since Cliff couldn't run and the last thing you wanted was a double play. But I love Willie for not managing like a card counter in Vegas. He manages human beings. He dreamed of a Bobby Thompson moment in Cliff, in what would probably have been his last turn at bat as a Met. It didn't happen. What the hell difference does it make? Would those of us who criticize him bitterly have praised him for being a genius if Cliff had hit a home run?

They lost. They didn't choke. There was nothing mediocre or gutless about the 2006 Mets. I am glad they didn't kick steps and water coolers. Bravely hopeful people who accept their failures accomplish more than people who kick and throw things. This is the way I'd want my daughter to react if she loses something. This is the way I want to react. And this is the way most Mets fans react because we don't have some Steinbrenner leading us, fat and stupid on the beach waving his arms and telling the waves to stop and that their disobedience is unacceptable.

My life would be poorer without the Mets. But my life would not have been one bit richer if the 1973 Mets had won the seventh game of the '73 Series. It wouldn't have been any better if the Mets had come back against the Dodgers to win the pennant in 1988. It wouldn't be richer if Kenny Rogers had not walked home the run that gave the Braves the 1999 National League pennant. And it wouldn't be any better if Carlos Beltran had caught the float of that beautiful curve ball and sent it to a place where everything is different.

The Point of Baseball

I love the game of baseball for itself. I love how it consists of protracted moments of confrontation that culminate in brief instants of action.

An "at bat" can last for minutes, during which, with your mind and your emotions, you are perpetually calculating and recalculating the probability of something you want to happen. Then, for a thrilling few seconds, the ball is in play and the "at bat" is given a permanent identity by what a few people, suddenly chosen by the event, do in a few seconds. What the batter has done, what the pitcher has done, and what the fielders and base runners do, has an impact on the growing and changing image you have of the players in your mind. Someone is coming out of a slump, someone can't hit or field, someone doesn't have it tonight, someone is the greatest player you have ever seen.

The "at bat" enters the eternal realm of numbers. What has just happened counts. It may determine who wins this game and who will win the division or the pennant this year. Because of what has just happened, the batter will always have one batting average and not another for this year. The batter's identity is now associated with the new numbers, leading you to project the numbers he will have at the end of the year.

What has just happened will affect what you feel about what can happen when the next batter comes to the plate, or when the batter who has just hit returns to the plate again. It may affect what you feel about the likely outcome of the game, or even the division or pennant race. An item of information that did not exist seconds ago has a vivid emotional meaning. The story of the game moves forward and now there is a new confrontation, which will, very soon, produce the excitement of the next quick and meaningful event.

So the game draws you in and moves you along as moments of tension are followed by moments of release, as speculation is followed by knowledge. It is as if you are riding along on a wave, feeling the unknown future becoming the vivid present and then taking permanent form as the past. In this way, watching baseball is like watching a movie or a play or reading a book. What is different is that those who are creating what you watch do not know what is coming any more than you do. The future is genuinely unknown and unknowable. There isn't even the thuggish certainty that a much stronger team will defeat a much weaker team. There is only a probability and in baseball no probability is a certainty. I can enjoy watching a game in which my team is 13 runs behind because I can feel that there is the possibility of something unprecedented: a 13-run comeback. It is not a probable event, but it is possible, in ways that it is not possible for a football team to come back from a 49-point deficit with two minutes left in the fourth quarter. As long as something is possible, there is hope, and as long as there is the most infinitesimal hope, there is baseball pleasure.

The pleasure of baseball, I think, depends entirely on the pleasure of hope. This may be why, for all my love of the beauties of the game, I can't actually enjoy watching a baseball game unless I care deeply about its outcome. I am also unable to enjoy the rebroadcast of a game whose outcome I know. There must be the uncertainty that gives every event its power and meaning. And there must be an emotional involvement with the fortunes of one team. Without either of these elements, watching a baseball game can be interesting, but that's all. Baseball has to be more than interesting. It has to be an emotional experience. You have to care. It's not enough to admire. And you have to care for the sheer pleasure of caring. You have to hope because it is fun to hope. Sure I care about the Mets and hope for their success. But to a certain degree, their success is beside the point. It is not more fun to be the fan of a successful team than an unsuccessful one. The point is the yearning. Winning is nice. But it is not the point.

Following Baseball

Despite the permanence of baseball in my life, most of my actual experience of baseball is intermittent and fragmentary. I listen to an inning or two on the radio or watch an inning or two on TV. If I am not very busy, or if I am driving somewhere or doing yard work at just the right time, or if a game is very important, I will watch or listen to most or all of a game. I don't catch every inning and neither do most fans. But I must keep in contact, I must know how they did, and I must know how everyone is doing.

I look at box scores and articles in newspapers and on the Web. I listen to sports talk shows. I must have an informed and detailed feeling about the team and everyone on it at every point during the season. I'm not entirely sure why I need to have this. I don't feel that it is essential for me to have an up-to-date informed response to whatever is happening, on a daily basis, in the lives of my friends. It seems all right to lose track for weeks or even months, in some cases years, and then to catch up.

But baseball is not a reality you can leave and return to. Unlike a person, it stops existing unless you "follow" it. It's a continuing narrative, like a book or a television serial. If you lose the thread, you've lost whatever it is. Fandom is following the thread, even if all that means is getting a score on the radio during an errand, or reading a box score after checking your e-mail.

So baseball is not just the pleasure of watching or hearing games or going to the stadium. It is also the pleasure of keeping the thing alive, the thing that is made of what happens in the games you could have heard but haven't. When you follow baseball it is real. It is a big grid with endless detail that can be gathered into numbers and rows of rankings. It changes every second and it grows and it morphs and it passes on and forward into the future. You ride on it as you would ride on the back of a great beast. You live it as you would live your life. Except you could make it all go away. You could make baseball disappear the way you make a dream disappear. It could become like the sports you don't follow, a mass of unknown detail, reported but unheard.

But if you made this dream go away, it would continue without you. You would busy yourself with whatever took you away from baseball. You would think it was gone. But then if you came back to it, it would pick you up again without saying anything about the fact that you were away.

Baseball and the Life of the Mind: Memories of Bart Giamatti

When I was in graduate school, I took a seminar on the English Renaissance poet Edmund Spenser. The seminar was taught by A. Bartlett Giamatti. Giamatti was a terrific teacher, animated, funny, and smart. As everyone at Yale knew, he loved baseball passionately, and every once in a while he would write a piece for a magazine about how something in baseball reminded him of something in Renaissance literature. In our oral presentations, those of us in the seminar who were baseball fans would often try to make some baseball analogy. Giamatti always appreciated this and he would commend us with a kind of "What the hell do you think you're doing?" look on his face.

One time, I saw Giamatti speak at a forum at Yale on baseball, with Roger Kahn and Ray Kroc. After the forum, he stood outside and talked with a few of us. It was baseball talk, the kind everybody does. We weren't trying to think of how you could compare baseball players to shepherds in pastoral poetry. After that, whenever I ran into Bart Giamatti on the Yale campus, which was actually quite often, he would stop and talk with me about baseball. He wanted to do it. I wouldn't have stopped him. Who knows how many people he did this with? I loved these talks on windy New Haven street corners. They weren't particularly necessary or deep. But they established a connection between us. On the day it was announced that Bart Giamatti was going to become the new president of Yale, I was so happy for him. I told a lunch table full of graduate students that I was sure that someday he would be the commissioner of baseball. I'm glad I did that. I have witnesses.

When I tell this story to people in the world outside of academics, they always want to turn it into something like "See, his real love was baseball." No, his "real" love wasn't baseball. He loved baseball and he loved Renaissance literature. Not only is there no contradiction here, there's a real connection. Both baseball and Renaissance literature are particularly appealing to people who have a lot of imagination.

Why is this? I have no idea. But what I am saying is true. Look at baseball blogs and compare them to football or hockey or basketball blogs. Even when they are focusing on the most arcane issue of strategy or statistical analysis, baseball fans are always looking for any excuse to break into their lyrical voice. They are all rank sentimentalists. They see a story in everything. Baseball, I actually believe, is less demanding intellectually, to follow or to play, than football, basketball, or hockey. But it is somehow friendlier to the fan's experience of contemplation. You can sit in the stands of a baseball stadium and realize things about your life, like what you want to do with yourself, or whether or not you want to have a kid, or whether to ask somebody to marry you. One of my favorite writers, Haruki Murakami, says that he decided to become a writer because one day, when he was 29, absorbed in his job and all of the details of ordinary life, he was sitting in the stands, drinking a beer, watching the Yakult Swallows playing the Hiroshima Carp. A player on the Swallows hit a double and Murakami decided that now it was time for him to write a novel. This is exactly right. This is why baseball is one of the greatest things there is. It is riveting, but it has pockets of time built into it, air bubbles that allow your emotions and your imagination to breathe.

I wish I could tell you something deep or revealing that Bart Giamatti told me about baseball. I can't. He loved the Red Sox. He wasn't crazy about George Steinbrenner and he was very unhappy when the Yankees signed Goose Gossage. I remember a few other things but none of them are anything other than what any Red Sox fan would have felt or said in the late 1970s. Giamatti was a fan. Which meant that he had his own personal relationship with baseball and yet what he thought and felt was pretty much the same as what everyone in the orbit of his team also felt and thought. This is why it was so great that he did become the commissioner of baseball. The commissioner should be a fan, someone who will fight for the fan. I was heartbroken when Bart Giamatti died after only five months as the commissioner. There was never going to be a fan's commissioner again. Giamatti was a fluke, a very lucky break. But he died of a heart attack when he was a year younger than I am now, died as I was driving down from Connecticut to New Jersey, listening to Mike and the Mad Dog who turned their whole show over to this horrible, unhappy event that ended this terrific story.

I have one more memory of Bart Giamatti. I was having an independent study session with J. Hillis Miller, the distinguished professor of Victorian literature who became my dissertation advisor. Giamatti came into Miller's office at the end of the session because they were going someplace together. "Oh, it's the Mets fan," Giamatti said and so we spent some time talking baseball with Hillis Miller, who was a fan of the Baltimore Orioles. They were telling me about their colleague Harold

Bloom and his passionate and tragic devotion to his Yankees. Only Bloom, they observed, could find and know the tragedy of being a Yankees fan. Anyway, the next day I was walking out of the Yale Library and I saw Miller approaching, with a friendly smile on his face. Beside him was a handsome white-haired man with pointy features, whom I recognized with a thrill of intense nervousness. J. Hillis Miller was about to introduce me to Jacques Derrida. If you know who Jacques Derrida is, you are wondering what the hell is going to happen. If you don't know who Jacques Derrida is, let me just say that he was one of the most influential intellectuals of the second half of the twentieth century, the central figure in something called deconstruction which ignorant journalists would ordinarily explain as a philosophical movement to drain the meaning and pleasure out of everything. It wasn't that, but now is not the time to explain what I think it was. Suffice it to say that Jacques Derrida had no interest at all in draining the meaning or pleasure out of anything.

So there we are, on a winter afternoon in New Haven, two extraordinarily important intellectuals and me. Miller is explaining to Derrida that I am, like Miller, and Giamatti, and Bloom, a big baseball fan. And so for the next five or six minutes, Miller and Derrida are both engaged in a strenuous effort (linguistically strenuous, as Derrida's spoken English wasn't very good) to explain to me what a big fan Derrida was of what Americans call soccer and the rest of the world calls football. I'm afraid I'm going to have to let you down here, too. I wish I could report to the world that we had, with our big minds, or at least with their big minds, expressed some insight into the pleasures of sports fandom that no one has ever had before. But we didn't. We were just, for that moment, some people talking about things we loved deeply. We knew that we didn't understand our love of sports any more than anyone else. But we were happy to stand out in the cold and enjoy and share the fact that we loved it.

Why Do We Do This to Ourselves?

Of all the things in my life, my involvement in baseball is the thing I understand the least. There are more important mysteries in my life than this. But none of them is as much of a mystery. I can give you a good reason why I am involved in everything else I am involved in. I can give you a good reason why I like or love everything else I like or love. I started off this book by saying that there is no good reason why I should care about the New York Mets. There is still no good reason. This book wasn't an effort to find the reason. It won't be found.

I won't lie to you. I like this. I like having something in my life that sits there like something in a dream. It feels as if it has a right to be here, but it doesn't. It doesn't care what I think. It doesn't care what suffering it causes me. It doesn't feel obligated to give me pleasure either. It's here. And it knows and I know that it is not going anywhere and there is nothing I can throw on it to make it die or disappear.

I don't really know if what I just said is true. Maybe baseball could finally piss me off enough to make it possible for me to get rid of it. But right now it sits there, with a big Mr. Mets head, funny but also a little scary, and with its big unmoving smile on its face, it looks as if it has no intention of ever leaving me alone. It's like something strange that came during one of my childhood birthday parties and never left when it was supposed to. It couldn't find its way out of the house and so now it is here forever.

It's like some very ancient god. It is an idol, with its own music and prayers. It brings a whole world with it and even though that whole world often looks perfectly sane (people hoping for the good fortune of a group of athletes, calmly assessing the chances of victory or discussing the merits of possible free agents) every once in a while you see some other side of it, some side where all of the people in the caps and jerseys are grinning skulls. It is like something out of *Ghostbusters*. It receives offerings, it fills you up and empties you. It is one of the oldest things in your head.

It is like other things that aren't exactly real but that you can't help but believe in.

I believe in it. And I am fascinated by the ancient thing. I respond to it immediately. The unfathomable attraction it has is the only justification for my interest. And since it can't really be put into words, I can't tell you the argument it is making. The other sports didn't get into me during my mental prehistory. As compelling as they are to others, they can never be real to me. I don't understand those who worship them. But when I see the exact color and script of Mets across the front of the uniform, when I see the word in print, when I see the logo, or the apple, or Shea at sunset, something happens. I am someplace I need to be. I am not brought back to 1962 or 1969 or 1986 or anything like that. I am brought to a place where everything Mets is there together, and all of the time is at the same time. All of the forty-five years. It is like some frightening heaven.

Being a Mets fan is not a choice I have made. So I can talk all I want about how it gives me a sense of community, how it is fun and interesting, how it is an exciting and beautiful thing to watch, how easy it is to become attached to all of the experiences and objects associated with it. All those things are important. But there is something else. Something with talons, something grandly beautiful, impossibly deep, and terrifying. Something that came to me in my dark room on hot summer evenings in the 1960s with the night winds blowing the curtains. Something that was in the faces of our old radios. It has, over time, driven me crazy and given me parcels of the purest happiness. It is something I can't explain, justify, or escape.

The Offseason

If the season doesn't ended with a ticker-tape parade, you feel, for the first few days, as if you were driving a speeding car that has gone off the road and is now on its back, with the wheels spinning. It takes a while for the wheels to stop spinning, for the adrenaline in your system to get back to a normal level.

Some fans, apparently, can start talking right away about trades and free agents and all that. I can't do it. I need some time to get used to the fact that the season is finally over, that nothing more can ever be added to it. It's as if someone you know has disappeared. Suddenly a constant background hum is silenced. You turn on the radio or the TV and the Mets are not there. It's as if some evil conspiracy has managed to eliminate all evidence that they ever existed.

Every so often during the offseason, you'll hit the WFAN button on your radio and hear the Schmooze talking about football, or Howie announcing a hockey game, or Gary announcing a basketball game. You feel as if you've caught them having an affair.

There is now the long, fitful, and boring night. You don't want to be outside. Soon, you forget what it was like, exactly, to have leaves on the trees and baseball on the radio.

Mets Fans Are Geeks: Forumworld and Blogosphere

During the offseason, the Mets do continue to exist on the Internet. Everything always exists on the Internet. It's a big soup made up of many obscure minds. In the 3-D world, the Mets are over for a while. But the Internet continues to dream them, over and over and over.

What was there before the Internet? Something they called the Hot Stove League, named after guys who sat around a hot pot-bellied stove in general stores in winter talking about their baseball teams. They still call baseball talk in the offseason the Hot Stove League, but the only thing that is hot is the laptop battery against the top of your thighs.

There will now always be an Internet and so what we are seeing is just the beginning. People in the future will probably have some kind of virtual reality apparatus that will enable them to slap hands with the people sitting beside them in the very realistic stands from which they watch the sixth game of the 1986 World Series in digitally remastered 3-D high definition. Who the hell knows what they will have in the future? I want to guess but I know I'd end up like the people in 1925 who guessed that there would be zeppelin ports on top of skyscrapers, or the people in 1965 who thought that highways in the year 2000 would be conveyor belts. Hey, people in 1965, there aren't any more Worlds Fairs and Shea is already being torn down! Yes, it certainly is amazing. And we still call the Mets amazing, like Stengel did. Isn't that cool? And guess what, they're building a new stadium that's little and looks just like Ebbets Field. Yes, a lot of people still live in New York. No, I'm sorry, I don't know why they're not building a bigger stadium. Yes, I know, I know.

I won't guess the future, but I will observe that we are at the beginning of it. Right now we have forums and blogs. I'm sure they'll have something like this a hundred years from now. The biggest forum is the Fan Forum on the official site, mets.com. This is like a mosh pit, or rather like a school lunchroom in the middle of a food fight with a few tables of people having serious conversations trying to ignore the food fight. Tens of thousands of people come here to share news (and hoaxes and lies) and feelings and observations. Some of them are kids who vomit and swear and don't pick up their beer cans. Some of them are morons who want the Wilpons' money to give them the illusion that they are leading some kind of triumphal existence. But most of the people who post here are smart and serious fans of the Mets, who don't live near a general store, but who want the human warmth there can be in the exchange of words and dreams. The metaphor in the name is a good one. This is a forum, where people talk and fight, where new saviors of the people are cheered, where there are victory marches and arches, and where the conquered are spared, the proud beaten down.

There are also smaller forums, like amazinz.com, grandslamsingle.com, and thehappyrecap.com, where grown-ups of all ages, sick of the food fight, try to find a place where they can write longer and more thoughtful posts and really get to know each other. These are quieter places, where people are given ranks depending on how many thousands of posts they've made, where they design elaborate signatures meant to serve as their faces, and where things are sometimes said about baseball that are deeper and richer than anything you will read in any book that anyone ever writes about it.

The best places for baseball on the Internet are the blogs, or at least the best of them. Some of the best have very basic names, like "Mets Blog" or "Mets Geek." Some of the best written have sentimentally suggestive names like "Take the 7 Train," "The Ed Kranepool Society," or "Faith and Fear in Flushing." Some of the blogs are jazzy and hot-shit clever, like "Hotfoot," "MetsGrrl," and "Metstradamus." Others are cozily personal like the thoughtful and penetrating "Mike's Mets." On blogs like these you will find detailed and analytical sports writing that is often better than what you can read in the newspapers. You can also learn something about how baseball connects to people's lives and hearts and souls and minds. Here is where you can see the great hunger people have for words about baseball that are not just the bland reporting and strategic analysis of a sports page. Here's where a door opens into the world where baseball really is.

In the future, there will be so much more than there is now. There will be more electronic things, and more ways to lose ourselves in words and images. But the thing at the center of baseball can't really change. There will have to be a game on a field, a game played between white lines in front of a curved fence, a game played on grass with bats and balls and bases, a game with certain rules that hook the mind and spirit in very specific ways. I am sure that whatever baseball is a hundred years from now, whatever differences there are in the way people make money and in the way images are sent and received, the game will still be something that would be as easy for me to recognize as the nineteenth-century game in "Casey at the Bat." There is an eternal form to baseball, because if it were to be changed in any fundamental way, it would lose its power. The essence of baseball cannot change. And the essence radiates outward from what is done on the field. Bats and balls will make their thumping and cracking sounds, curve balls will curve and sliders will do whatever they do, and it follows from this that there will always be peanuts and Cracker Jack, and gloves and hot dogs will always smell, and everyone will always sing at the seventh-inning stretch. Over all the centuries that have passed and are to come, what the crowd will feel when it leaps to its feet or takes the punch of a third strike in the stomach, won't be any different from what you and I have felt in our few decades with all of this fun.

The Return of Baseball

Over the winter, I will follow the signings and trades. The drugstores will turn orange and black, then red and green, then red and pink. And just when I am beginning to feel that there never was such a thing as baseball, pitchers and catchers will report to camp in Florida. In the papers, I will see pictures of players on a field, doing stretches in warm sunlight. For me, it will still be cold outside. But the cold night without baseball will be over.

Nothing much happens in camp in February, but there will be interviews and features anyway. If something does happen, if someone says something stupid, or is late for practice, it will be blown up out of proportion. Everyone will be eager for something to happen. But nothing will happen. Still, I will read every word of the articles as religiously as if it were October and the Mets were in the playoffs.

Then, on a weekend in early March, I will hear the voices again, the ones that always awaken me from my winter slumber. I will hear the familiar songs, the old commercials, the new commercials, and all the sounds of a game. I will hear the new names, of the guys who will soon be cut, and I dream of their future. I will remember hearing other names for the first time. I will imagine that I can tell something from the first winter at-bats. I will try to read the tea leaves.

There aren't many good reasons to listen to or watch an exhibition game. But I will do it anyway and I will enjoy it. By late March, I will be asking: "Aren't they ready yet? Haven't they done this before? Do they really need this much time?" Finally the rosters and lineups will be set. A couple of games against rivals will seem kind of real but not real enough. When the season is finally ready to start, I will be more than ready. I will feel as if I've earned the warm air and the meaningful games.

I will be rewarded with Opening Day and all of its momentous pageantry. Players will line up on the sidelines. I will cheer and get a lump in my throat. The first game will begin and I will marvel that the at-bats actually count and will live forever in the statistics. I will forget all of the good years that began badly and all the bad years that began well. After all the late winter dreaming, I will be so anxious for real baseball that I will have forgotten how little a single game, a single clutch hit, a single botched relief appearance, really means. It does not mean more, just because I am paying more attention, as I savor the first sweet drops I squeeze from the season.

As April moves towards May, I still won't know what is real and what isn't. The fielders' hands will still be cold. Some of the pitchers will be getting nervous looking for their rhythm. Some of the batters will take advantage and others won't. The batting averages of the league leaders will be ridiculous. Some teams will have winning streaks and I will make little changes to my pre-season predictions. Soon enough, most of the obscure names will fall from their positions at the top of the leaders' lists. The standings will no longer look as if they have been shuffled by a crazy person. The season's one or two real surprises will settle into substance. The rest of the anomalies will drop like cartoon characters, when they finally realize they've run off the end of the cliff.

The leaves will be back on the trees. The articles will have better information, but I won't read them with as much urgency. I will forget that there was so recently a time without baseball and without leaves. I will be in the middle of it all over again.

Groundbreaking Ceremonies for Citi Field

Three weeks after the 2006 baseball season ended, a name was given to the new Mets stadium that will open in April of 2009. The name "Citi Field," marking a deal with CitiGroup, was announced at an official groundbreaking ceremony. My first reaction to the name was horror. "No Way!" I thought, "I'm not calling it that! I'll cut my tongue out first!" I calmed down after a few hours. So what if it has a corporate name? Were they going to give up 20 million dollars a year to keep a commercial out of the name? It could have been a lot worse. Citi Field isn't that bad, although it will always be easy for our adversaries to call it "Shitti Field." But this is okay. They weren't going to call it Bob Murphy stadium. Or Doris from Rego Park stadium. That's not the way things work.

I think my relationship to Citi Field right now is like a kid's relationship to an appealing new stepparent. I am looking for reasons to hate it because I know I will have to end up loving it because, whether I want it or not, it will become a very important part of my life. I don't like how small it is. I think there's going to be real trouble if the Mets stay good and it becomes impossible for ordinary people without season plans to get a ticket. Yeah, I guess that there are ways in which they can add more seats if it becomes a problem. I worry that it is going to be too slick, and that all of the appealing tackiness of Shea will be scrubbed out. This would change forever what it is to be a Mets fan. Hey, will you still be able to see the green tower and the U-Haul sign? What if you can't?

Knowing that Citi Field was going to become part of my life, I recorded the official groundbreaking ceremonies on SNY. When I got home from work, I played back what my system recorded in the scheduled slot, from 11 to 12. There were Chuck Norris and Christie Brinkley and a bunch of people with nice bodies selling gym equipment. There was a banner across the bottom that said that the Mets' groundbreaking ceremonies were coming up. They finally started, a half an hour late.

The ceremony started, as such things do, with the introduction of officials and politicians. The politicians are supposed to speak first. You know, it would be great if politicians understood that part of their job is to focus people's emotions, to get people to feel the significance of an event. Look at what Lincoln did at Gettysburg. Would George Pataki, Sheldon Silver, and Michael Bloomberg offer what we needed at this far less demanding event? Do you have to ask?

Pataki spoke first. He said in 1957 he wasn't "exactly broken-hearted" to see the Dodgers and the Giants leave New York. Yet he was glad when National League baseball came back to New York and he says that he used to love to go to the Polo Grounds and watch Choo Choo Coleman, Rod Kanehl, and Jay Hook (why those three? why those three?) "losing just about every game they played." Great line, George! Well, Mr. Smartypants-I-know-my-audience-and-I-have-them-in-the-palm-of-my-hand goes on to observe that even if the Mets weren't so hot back then, he fell in love with Mets fans because of how loudly they'd cheer a Met getting a walk in the eighth inning even though the team was fifteen runs behind. Yeah, George, we're still like that. We still win about 40 games per year and we still cheer walks when we're 15 runs behind. But the great thing about the team, the governor observes, is that they wanted to "reclaim a little of the glory," so they brought over a former Yankee to manage the team! Casey Stengel! And now, more recently, they again tried to "reclaim the glory" by bringing in another Yankee to manage the team, Willie Randolph! Claps and cackles all around. So, as George deftly understands, the Mets and Mets fans like to be understood in the context of the Yankees. We're the same old loveable bunch of numbskulls we were in 1962, adorably choosing the wrong team to root for. But he's looking forward to, guess what? Another Subway Series! Wouldn't that be great for the great great State of New York?

Sheldon Silver, the speaker of the assembly, then got up and wondered if his disagreements with George Pataki could be traced back to the fact that Pataki was a Yankees fan growing up and Silver was a Dodgers fan. Okay, here's something interesting. The Dodgers championed civil rights and the Yankees ignored it while it was happening. Rachel Robinson is sitting right there on the podium. The Mets have announced that there will be a Jackie Robinson rotunda (a consolation prize because Rachel couldn't cough up the $20 million a year it would have taken to beat out CitiGroup). This will give the Mets a claim to an admirable aspect of the Dodger's legacy. Well, does old Dodgers fan Sheldon Silver bleed orange and blue? It doesn't look like it. He asks us what we remember about the seventh game of the NLCS. Do we remember that the Cardinals won? Yes. Or (pause for emphasis) do we remember the catch made by Endy Chavez? Sheldon, the accent is on the first not the second syllable and that is a "ch" as in "cheese-y," not a "sh" as in Sheldon. You don't remember anything about that game do you? As it happens, we Mets fans remember both of these things, and we know that we don't have a choice between them.

Then it was the turn of the mayor of the greatest city in the world. Thank you for a great season, he says pleasantly. He has to root for both New York teams, he tells us. Why? Giuliani didn't feel he needed to. You grew up in Brookline, Mike, root for the Red Sox. Nobody's going to care. But he tells us later in his speech that he doesn't really remember if he was a Red Sox or a Braves fan. It's funny how you forget stuff like that. Bloomberg doesn't have much to say. He does point out that he didn't know baseball team owners or baseball players when he was growing up. That's interesting. Oh, and he points out that he admires athletes, like his daughter (apparently she rides a horse) and like the Mets in the audience because they strive to be the best at what they do. He couldn't do what they do. But he tries to be the best at what he does. Well, anyway.

The next four people who spoke only had about a minute each to observe that the stadium would be good for the community and create thousands of jobs.

Then our owner Fred Wilpon came up and began with a story about him and his wife and barely pre-natal son Jeff being at the groundbreaking ceremony for Shea. Then he started his remarks and my recording of the groundbreaking shut off.

I realize that this may not be a fair account of what happened. I'm sorry. I was in a really foul mood watching this. I am glad that this project will give work to so many. But building a new sewer system would also create a lot of jobs.

This is a cathedral that is being built. And the old cathedral has to be torn down. This is a beautiful and terrifying moment. In other civilizations it would have called for the sacrifice of animals or even people. Maybe an epic poem. My DVR has reached the end and it has begun to play the recorded hour from the beginning. I pause it. Christie Brinkley looks like she's about to say something. Chuck Norris looks puzzled. I want more. But I really have no idea what I have the right to ask for.

Senseless change is awful. Sensible change can be worse. There is nothing you can say. You have no power to preserve what you have always had and you have no right to remain as you have always been.

The Mets in the Future

Now is as good a time as any to be nostalgic. We are at a moment in Mets history that will, in the future, be comparable to the place held by the birth of Christ in the way in which we count the years. B.C. Before Citi Field. C.E. Citi Field Era. The old home, the old thing that Robert Moses hoped would resemble the Roman Coliseum, and perhaps last as long, is about to be torn down.

I look at the new thing on the Web. On the Mets site, there's a fly-through, that allows you to glide through the new stadium as if you were what you are, a ghost from the past, someone who has only known Shea, who is swimming through the ether unseen by people going to a game at Citi Field, which is to them what Shea is to us. The medium through which you appear to swim is blurry and shimmery. The people you pass by and over are not moving. So it seems as if you are in one of these moments in an old sitcom where everyone has been frozen by a spell. Their features are indistinct. It's like they're mannequins. But you aren't supposed to notice them. They are just there to suggest that there will be people in the new stadium. Still, you can't help but be freaked out by them because this is what the people of the future are in relationship to you. They don't exist, but when they do exist, you won't exist.

Anyway, first you glide in from on high, as if you were dropping from the heavens. The city has been blurred out and all you see is the stadium and the parking lot. What happened to the city, to Corona Park, to the ruins of the Fair? Will they have these things in the future? This isn't the distant future. The jerseys people are wearing say Martinez and Reyes. But how can the near future possibly look like this?

You approach the front with its grand Romanesque arches. This is very impressive. Then you glide along the side and you see people on balconies and then down on a plaza. You enter a big rotunda that has lamp posts and hanging chandeliers like the atrium of the old Paris Opera House, which is appropriate because at this point you feel like the Phantom of the Opera. You glide up the escalators and there is an inscription from Jackie Robinson. Are you in the Lincoln Memorial? Are you in Grand Central Station? No, here you go, you enter the stadium. There it all is. It looks like an old ballpark, not like a new one. Pretty but soundless. Retro immaculate. It looks like a three-dimensional drawing made of pixels which is of course what it is. You don't hear the planes or smell the hot dogs. And the people are still mannequins. Will you be waking up soon? Will they start to see you?

You suddenly find yourself gliding with the same smooth but hysterical speed over the Mets dugout and through the field boxes. Then you go up a level and glide around the horseshoe from that height. Then you go out on the field. Things are happening very quickly now, and you feel as if you're a whirling dervish. It is ending now and you are rising up higher and higher above the stadium. You look down. What is that eerily empty thing? Oh my God, suddenly it is filled with people. There is the crowd, like sparkling pebbles.

If I live a long time, I will be one of the last people who will be able to say that they have been fans of the New York Mets for their entire history. I will be one of the last people who will be able to say that he has seen a Mets game in the Polo Grounds, in Shea Stadium, and in Citi Field. If Citi Field lasts just as long as Shea and if I live into my nineties, I will have a shot at seeing a game in the fourth stadium as well. There will be a fourth stadium. And a fifth someday. And more. It is like all the layers of Troy.

As I write this at the end of 2006, the Mets have not won a World Series in twenty years. They might have won one this year, but in the end they didn't. Maybe they'll win one next year. Maybe, even if they're good, they'll never win one again in my lifetime. My best guess is that they'll win a World Championship one or two more times. Three would be great. Five is unlikely. There is going to be a lot more disappointment than triumph. You can count on that. But it will never not be fun. The Yankees, as they may have told you, have something like 26 World Series rings. They think they're rich. But that's like thinking you're rich because you have a lot of play money.

I am rich. For all of my pain and sorrow, for all of my bitching and moaning, for all of my fear and nausea, I've got what I want. I've got them. I've got the Mets.

Index